ב״ה

The Power
of
Choice

A PRACTICAL GUIDE TO CONSCIOUS LIVING
Based on Kabbalah & Torah Wisdom

☐ ☑

RAV DOVBER PINSON

IYYUN
PUBLISHING

IYYUN PUBLISHING

Published by IYYUN Publishing
232 Bergen Street
Brooklyn, NY 11217

http:/www.iyyun.com

Iyyun Publishing books may be purchased for educational, business or sales promotional use. For information please contact: contact@IYYUN.com

cover and book design: RP Design and Development

pb ISBN 978-0-9914720-1-7

Pinson, DovBer 1971-
The Power of Choice: A Practical Guide to Conscious Living, Based on Kabbalah & Torah Wisdom
1.Judaism 2. Spirituality 3. Self-Help

This book is dedicated to

REB LAZER SCHEINER שיחי׳

together with

his wife, Heather שתחי׳
& their children שיחיו׳

MAY THEY BE BLESSED WITH *Shefa*
— AN ABUNDANT STREAM —
OF PHYSICAL, MATERIAL AND SPIRITUAL WEALTH
IN A REVEALED AND EXPANSIVE WAY.

We can either control
or be controlled
by our circumstances.

When we choose to choose
we lay claim to our life.

CONTENTS

THE POWER OF CHOICE

CONTENTS

THE POWER OF CHOICE

OPENING

_____

*Acknowledging
the Obstacles*

◻◻

You can't control
what life throws at you,

but you can control
what you throw back

THE POWER OF CHOICE

□□

The ability for each one of us to tune in to our own unique voice and perspective takes time to develop. There are so many competing agendas and contradictory voices vying for our attention. It is often quite difficult to quiet down the storm long enough to hear that still small voice inside communicating to each of us our unique purpose and true desire.

It is the ability to honestly observe our unconscious patterns and to ask ourselves the tough questions that enables us to acknowledge and articulate our soul's wildest dreams.

Everyone wants the best for themselves, but sadly, all too often people get deflated and defined by their own sense of smallness. As a result, we frequently find ourselves tangled up in psychological spider webs of nonsense. We tend to sabotage our own lives.

Based on the positive perspective that a better life is possible and that we are often all that is standing in our own way, the burning question then becomes: How do we untangle ourselves from this mess of our own making? How do we hit the personal reset button to start all over again so that we can feel more alive, in-spired, focused and present in the moment? How do we overcome anger, let go of guilt, process our paranoia and focus our desires in a healthy way?

The teachings collected here deal primarily with these basic life questions — questions we all have about how best to deal with life and its challenges. It is the essential contention of this book that we do indeed hold the key to unlock many of the gates that are holding us back and keeping us from the proverbial garden.

That key is the power to choose.

The power of choice requires conscious awareness, including the ability to honestly reflect upon one's options and identity. It is the primary tool that we as humans have at our disposal to impact the world and effect change within our own lives. Too often do we give this power up to outside forces such as the market, media, politicians or peer pressure; or to internal forces that often func-tion beyond our conscious control such as ego, anger, lust, greed or jealousy. The power of choice is our psychological "pause" or "reset" button. It is our ability to not just go with the flow if that flow is taking us somewhere we do not want to go. The power of choice gives us the opportunity to plot our own course and to find the flow which moves in that direction.

Making conscious, compassionate and creative decisions is the cornerstone of the art of living a mature and meaningful life. This ability to curate and craft our environment and experience is quite possibly the defining feature of a human being, "made in the Cre-ator's image." And yet, this fundamental act, this Divinely given evolutionary birthright, is often atrophied for lack of adequate use. Most of us are regretfully resigned and have simply surrendered ourselves to the way we "are" or to the way the world "works." This leads to an underlying feeling of defeat and inevitable failure before we even try to do something different or achieve something amazing. So many of us have simply given up our power to choose.

This book seeks to return that power to its rightful wielder— you.

LAYING THE FOUNDATION
FOR SPIRITUAL GROWTH

□□

Within the genre of self-help literature, and spiritual wisdom in general, there are ethical teachings designed to help one become a better member of collective society. These kinds of teachings seek to ensure that one is in healthy balance and relationship with other people and with all of life. This strain of teaching is designed to help one become what is referred to in Yiddish as a *mensch*—a good-natured, well-mannered, caring and compassionate person.

Additionally, there are teachings and practices that help to focus and expand one's awareness and intention in order to develop and maintain their connection with their deepest, truest self. These types of teachings are designed to refine our sense of inner consciousness. This strain of teaching is intended to help one become what is referred to in Hebrew as a *chassid*—a pious, passionate, positive and poetic person.

These two approaches to self-improvement address both our external relationships with others as well as our own internal experiences on the rollercoaster of life. When these approaches are combined, one is able to respectfully relate to what can be referred to as the "I" and the other "I." The first "I" in this equation refers to our inner sense of subjectivity; while the other "I" is manifest within the fully granted subjectivity of the other whom we encounter in mutual dialogue and meaningful relationship. These two paths comprise the fundamental basics of personal growth and refinement. This is practical wisdom, addressing mainly our social and psychological realities, without the slightest hint of metaphysics or cosmology.

In the words of the Jewish sages of old: "*Derech Eretz*/ethical and moral behavior precedes *Torah*/spiritual practice." Ethical and moral behavior (i.e. derech eretz) is the foundation for any path of deeper and higher spiritual development. Before one can climb a ladder, one must make sure that the ladder is firmly grounded. And that is precisely what this book is about: establishing the basic groundwork for sustainable personal growth. In other words, this is the pre-requisite coursework before signing up for Spirituality or Kabbalah 101. No higher-level classes are recommended until these lessons are digested and integrated in a real and demonstrable way.

Within oneself—and indeed within all of reality—there are physical, emotional, mental and spiritual dimensions. It is ill advised for one to attempt to leap-frog to the "spiritual" realms before being able to secure oneself within the physical, emotional and mental dimensions first.

The physical dimension refers to our actual embodied behavior. This is the very ground upon which the ladder of spiritual development is placed. Included in this stage of development are the most basic precepts governing good health, such as; proper eating, sleep and exercise, as well as relational principles that guide our interpersonal interactions including family, physical intimacy and society. Much of this wisdom is contained within the Torah itself as found within the laws of commerce, familial relations and various other practical methods and means of caring for and building a just society and purified physical vessel.

We should ideally have a firm grasp on what is healthy for our own particular physical makeup, as well as what is productive for the specific society we find ourselves in before embarking on the next stage of holistic human development (i.e. the more internal, mental and emotional realms, which is where this book will begin from). It is precisely here that we are able to encounter and confront our own appetites, passions, perspectives and decision-making processes in order to refine them. As mentioned, work on this level should be viewed as laying the foundation for deeper, inner spiritual work.

Therefore, this book aims to focus our attention on mental and emotional practices and perspectives that enable us to exercise our power to choose a better tomorrow for ourselves in the present moment.

EVERY PART AFFECTS THE WHOLE

□□

In truth, everything we do, say or even think has repercussions on all levels of being. Every one of our actions, words or thoughts affects, either positively or the opposite, our relationship with our own deepest self, with those around us, and with the world as a whole.

Every action or inaction can either lead to connection or disconnection, bonding or alienation, creation or destruction. This dynamic is hinted at within the three root-letters of the Biblical Hebrew word for 'choice,' *bechira*, as these three letters can be reconfigured to form the word *chaver*, the Hebrew word for 'friend' or 'connection,' as well as the Hebrew word *chorav*, 'to destroy.' We can learn from these psycho-linguistic hints encoded within the ancient Hebrew language that every life-choice we make can either enhance or destroy our connection with others, with ourselves, with life in general and with our Creator.

Every positive action—thought or word—has the power to create a *yichud*/unification on all levels of our being, which in turn ripples outward to positively affect the whole world around us.

Conversely, when we inflict harm—be it physical, emotional or mental—on another human being, or for that matter upon ourselves, we are destroying and separating ourselves from our own higher potential and purpose of being. In so doing we are creating a kind of barrier between our deepest, realest self and others.

When we become a more conscious and caring person it is not only good for us, it is good for everyone and everything around us.

All of our energies are contiguous and contagious, affecting all that falls within our sphere of influence.

We all have the innate ability to live bigger, happier, more expansive and productive lives. We all have the capacity to live from the place of our perfection. It is every human's birthright to manifest their deepest and highest physical, emotional, mental and spiritual potential.

When we are able to live this way, we inspire others to do the same. This is the cosmic domino effect in which each piece either supports or topples the other pieces in its vicinity.

When we activate and animate our highest Self, we become a perfect and transparent mirror; reflecting back to all who look in our direction their own potential to be great as well.

You know that you are living your highest purpose and potential when you are making those around you feel better about their own lives as well. The sure sign of a truly great person is one who inspires greatness in others. When we meet a true leader or teacher we can actually feel their empowerment and expansiveness, it rubs off on us, giving us a kind of contact high. This is in contrast to those leaders or teachers who seek to control you, by making you feel diminished or less adequate in order to make themselves feel greater and more powerful.

This is a good barometer to know when you are manifesting your deepest self: If you are lifting up the people around you, if your presence and process makes them feel bigger and better about themselves, then you are surely manifesting your highest and purest potential.

ACKNOWLEDGING THE OBSTACLES:

————

Thinking Too Small

&

Thinking Too Big

□□

Before we go any further, it is important to consider two very common pitfalls along the path of self-development. One pitfall is thinking too big, and the other is thinking too small.

When many of us look at our lives, we may experience a feeling of general malaise, unhappiness, boredom or even despair, and thus feel the need to make drastic changes in order to balance out our negative existential equation. Often, our thinking goes something like this: "If I feel this bad, then I need to do something equally exceptional to make myself feel that good."

And so we dream big and shoot for the stars. This is not a bad thing in and of itself. However, if you really want to reach the stars you are going to have to do more than jump. You're going to have to take a billion baby-steps to make that quantum leap. And this is precisely where so many of us get caught up. We set our sights too high without giving ourselves any concrete, gradual or attainable milestones to mark our progress along the way towards our ultimate goal.

For example, a person may want to become a better father, mother, spouse or friend; so they say to themselves, "I am going to be the best father or mother in the world," or, "I am going to be the best husband" or the "best wife ever." While these are nice sentiments they usually amount to nothing more than some shallow displays of exaggerated niceties, such as spending a single weekend of quality time with one's child or buying a nice gift for one's spouse, before ultimately reverting back to old habits. Although these resolutions are often genuine, and they do express positive aspirations, hardly anything ever comes from these kinds of declarations because they are just too general and abstract. Eventually, after experiencing the frustration of not magically achieving the goal of being the champion at whatever it was we were aiming for, most of us will simply go back to our old patterns of behavior. These lofty goals set us up for defeat and leave us with little to no consolation or way of gauging our gradual progress.

Real change takes real work. Real work requires realistic goals. Realistic goals result from a functional understanding of our inner reality.

In short: Habits are not easily changed, and ultimately, grandiose resolutions are not the answer.

To effectively transform ourselves at our core we need to rewire the brain and set new patterns of behavior.

One way to achieve this is through consistent, seemingly small actions.

A small act can be a goal that we set with regular reminders such as saying to ourselves, "today, when I come home from work I will give my child fifteen uninterrupted minutes of my time before doing anything else." Or, "next time I go out with my friends or family I will not look at my phone."

These small actions, when repeated consciously, eventually rewire our brain and become second nature. Additionally, they provide us with tangible touchstones that enable us to gauge our progress. The feeling of accomplishment that we experience after a solid month of achieving a set of small goals provides us with a great boost of inspiration and encouragement to take our personal growth to the next level.

□□

Now, let's address the opposite issue — setting our sights too low.

Sometimes we get so lost in the details of our lives that we lose sight of the bigger picture. In this way, we become disconnected from our truest passions and potentials and end up going around and around in the same unconscious loops and patterns that keep us running in place, so to speak.

Alternatively, some of us get so used to our own mediocrity or fear of failure that we find it hard to accept that an amazing opportunity has been presented to us. Over the years, many of us have developed a psychological narrative in which we lose every time. In this way we have pre-determined the outcomes of our efforts before we even begin. This blinds us to unexpected blessings that are positively out of the ordinary. How many opportunities do we miss by simply not recognizing them when they present themselves?

Or, there are those of us who get so lost within our own immediate appetites or unconscious reactions, that we just cannot hold it together long enough for something beyond our expectations to occur. Sometimes the treasure that we have spent so long seeking is just one more step away, and we just need to exercise some self-discipline in order to attain our goal. We need to be able to respond to our appetites in healthy ways, while at the same time seeing them within a bigger picture and process. Although the colloquial saying, "a bird in hand is worth two in the bush," is often true, there are crucial moments when our decisions and discipline (or lack thereof) may determine whether we get to eat a fish in the moment or learn to fish for the future.

In so many ways so many people set their sights so low that they are simply incapable of taking advantage of huge opportunities that may come their way.

By only focusing on the most immediate aspects of their life, they effectively create their own limitations and narrow their view of what is possible. In this way they become enslaved to their small-picture vision of life. This is similar to an elephant that is sadly raised in captivity. If a chain is placed on the elephant's leg as a baby, then even after the elephant has grown into a mighty animal, it still thinks it cannot detach from the chain, even though it could easily break free with the slightest pull of its leg.

To illustrate with an example:

One day, a homeless man who was down on his luck was sitting on a park bench. He just found a half-eaten hotdog in the trash and was right about to have his lunch when he hears his name being called. He looks up from his hotdog and finds himself face to face with an old friend and prior work partner. His old friend, dismayed at his condition, begins asking him about his life. After a few minutes of talking, and out of a genuine desire to help, the old friend offers the homeless man a job and a place to stay while he gets back on his feet. At that very moment, a cat climbs up on the park bench and starts sniffing at the hotdog. As they are talking about this amazing life-changing opportunity, all the homeless man can think about is shooing the cat away to save his hotdog. Finally, the cat makes a swipe and snatches the hotdog out of the man's hand and runs away. Without thinking the man jumps up and chases the cat through the park, winding this way and that between trees and bushes, running through ponds and jumping over flower beds. The cat is too quick for him and eventually he throws up his hands in despair and gives up. Just then he remembers, "Oh my G-d! My friend. The job! A house! What am I doing chasing after this cat for a half-eaten hotdog?!" He hurries back to the park bench, but by the time he arrives his old friend is gone. The opportunity has passed, just like that.

Obviously, this is an extreme case used to illustrate a point. But, truthfully, we all have our own challenges and appetites that exert control over us, blinding us to imminent opportunities and holding us back from real change in our lives. The homeless man's predicament symbolizes whatever you are going through that you desperately want to shift or grow out of. The hotdog represents whatever tiny, or insignificant benefits you are able to receive while still in your situation. The man's friend represents the opportunity to quantum leap out of your situation into a completely different reality. And the cat symbolizes the temptation or distraction that keeps you stuck in your conditioned behavior patterns, not allowing you to stay the course long enough to evolve in the direction that is ultimately best for you. The cat keeps you in the bag, so to speak.

Another example:

Once in Russia there was a simple soldier who performed a heroic act in battle and saved the life of Nicholas I. When he was granted a private audience with the king he was told that he could ask for absolutely anything and his wish would be granted. When he was brought in front of the king, he only requested that the king change his supervising officer.

Instead of seeking a promotion to become the supervising officer, he chose to remain a simple soldier and merely asked for a different commander. This poor soldier was operating within a limited reality. In his eyes, he was a mere foot soldier who needed to follow orders and was not able to think of himself as a supervisor capable of giving orders to others. He did not have the power or perspective to dream of bigger and better things for himself. If he only desired, he could have seized the opportunity and asked to become the commanding officer himself. Instead he missed his opportunity and only sought to better his standing within his very small sphere.

This type of constricted thinking affects us all, at one point or another. Many times we find ourselves in situations that trap us and limit our vision of what is possible. We get stuck in a certain rut and do not have either the stamina or the foresight to attempt a move. This happens in relationships, in jobs, and in countless other crucial areas of our life. What is worse, studies suggest that up to 90% of our thoughts during the day are the same thoughts we had the day before. Is it any wonder then, that progress seems so hard to come by?

Even more challenging is the fact that it is often not the *situations* themselves that trap us, but it is *we alone* who throw ourselves into psychological prisons of our own design. In this way we unconsciously choose to be confined and constricted. How many times after doing something a certain way and then being told that there is an easier, faster or better way to do it, do we still follow the old ways in which we already accustomed to?

To counteract this pattern of thinking it is important that you allow yourself to dream and think big, in order to open yourself up to blessings beyond belief. Do not forget the bigger picture by losing yourself within the myriad of insignificant details that too often distract you from your real goal. Sometimes it is necessary to give up on an immediate satisfaction in order to maintain the momentum to move you towards your desired destination. The marathon itself is what gives each step its meaning and direction. One must never lose sight of the finish line.

In either case, whether thinking too big or too small, the challenge is yours to overcome. You have the power to choose how to act, or react, in the long and short run. True, we are hardwired to behave in mostly unconscious ways, running most of the time on autopilot; but now that you know there is a different way, it is up to you to do what is necessary to get to where your heart wants to take you. The choice is yours.

Let us begin.

□□

Live from the inside-out
and choose how you are going to feel.

Live from the outside-in
and other people
will choose for you.

LIVING

IN THE IMAGE OF THE CREATOR:

———

Being the Cause of Your Life

□□

I n life, you can see yourself as a determining factor or as an already determined outcome. This is the fundamental choice we all have to make: we can either be the cause/creator of our life or we can be the effect/creation of what happens to us. In other words, we can live from the inside-out (cause/creator) or from the outside-in (effect/creation).

Each individual experiences life in two simultaneous realities; the outer world and the inner world. Broadly speaking, the outer world is what comes into us through our senses — what we see, hear, touch, taste or smell. Our inner world is how we process, think and feel about these sensations. In simplified terms - the outer world is the world of *what* and the inner world is the world of *how*.

There is *what* you eat; this is very important. But equally important is *how* you eat. Do you eat with awareness or with abandon? Do you eat to live or do you live to eat? The *what* determines what you put into your mouth, the *how* determines how you chew, digest and integrate it.

Living as if you were the effect of your life, means that your external circumstances dictate your internal state of mind. This perspective implies that your inner life is solely the effect of all the outside 'causes' you encounter.

Living as a 'creator' or cause of your life means that you decide how you are going to feel and live; you become the cause of your own life, not just the effect of a random set of circumstances.

In order to simplify this idea, and provide an example from day-to-day life, let's say that you wake up in the morning and it is rainy and gloomy outside. Do you automatically feel depressed? If so, you are approaching life from the outside-in, as an effect, rather than a cause of your reality. In this scenario, the weather is dictating how you are going to feel. The same is true, if you wake up in the morning and the sun is shining and you think to yourself, "today is going to be a great day!" Again, the outside world is dictating how you are going to feel internally. But if you wake up in the morning and declare: "Today is going to be a great day - rain or shine!"- you are choosing, and by extension, creating your day. You are thus the cause/creator of how your day is going to be, no matter what happens.

When we surrender our freewill, to the circumstantial sensory stimulus of the outside world, then we live our life as a mere effect.

However if we live our life from the inside-out, it is we who choose *how* we are going to deal with what we encounter and experience. Our inner world becomes an active participant in the larger context of the life in which we exist.

The weather is an obvious example. There are multiple other illustrations of the difference between living from the outside-in versus from the inside-out. For instance, there are people who must endure some form of personal tragedy in order for them to develop a more compassionate side of their personality. Additionally, there are those who must be showered with love and acceptance in order for them to feel open and confident. Similarly; there are people that need to be smiled at in order for them to smile; such people need to be complimented to feel good about themselves, and conversely they feel down when they are criticized. These are all instances of living from the outside–in.

Then there are people who live from the inside-out—they choose to be compassionate, they choose to show love or be friendly, regardless of what is happening around them. Such people choose how they are going to interact with others and do not wait to first see how others will interact with them. They are living as the cause of their life, and on account of their self-generated love and positivity, people around them respond in kind. This relational mirroring dynamic is expressed poetically in the Biblical teaching, "as water reflects the face, so too does the heart of man to man" *(Proverbs, 27:19).*

We are all gifted with a Spark of the Creator, this is our soul, a Divine inheritance that gives each of us the ability to become co-creators of our own lives. We may not control what life places before us, such as if it is sunny or rainy or whether another person insults or praises us, but we do have the power to choose how we are going to inwardly process and respond to such external stimuli. When we make conscious decisions we activate the Divine gift of freewill and become the cause of our life. We are, in that moment, choosing how we are going to live our life, no matter what.

Let us all choose to become empowered co-creators of our lives and not helpless victims of blind circumstance.

◻◻

Past is Memory.
Future is Fantasy.
The only real moment
is Now.

Be Present in the Present.

LIVING IN THE PRESENT

□□

S o much of our time is spent reminiscing about the past or worrying about the future that very little time is spent being present in the moment. Far too much of our energy is spent thinking about what has already occurred or what could possibly be, rather than focusing on what is happening now. A moment in which we divert our attention back into the past, or project it into the future, is a moment stolen from the present, robbing us of the extraordinary opportunity to make each moment special, unique and meaningful.

The mind tends to move in many directions at once, often spreading itself thin in the moment, as it is habitually drawn back into the past or forward into the future. Even, and especially, when we actively want and attempt to settle into the present moment there is so much distraction. This is certainly true for the current generation as the social environment is claustrophobic with the continuous stimulus of iPhones, iPads and all forms of gadgetry. With all of these digital distractions, combined with our predilection for dallying in the distant past or frolicking in the foggy future, our awareness is in constant danger of becoming so dispersed that we miss the miracle of the present moment.

Generally speaking, the future fills us with anxiety while the past stirs up regret. The mind spins out of control as it confronts the ultimate unknowability of the future, asking itself unanswerable questions, such as: "Will I have enough money?," "Will I be healthy?," "Will I find love?" and so on. So many choices we make today are based on imaginary predictions that we paint for ourselves about the future. Similarly, the mind gets stuck in the quicksand of the past, as it perpetually replays events looking for alternative outcomes. Every misstep is over-analyzed, crippling us in the present for fear of making the wrong decision based on our faulty track-record. So much of our mind-set today is founded on the choices, good or bad, that we made yesterday.

Strictly speaking, we cannot return to the past nor exist in the future at all; it is an existential impossibility. Any 'past' or 'future' that we could—theoretically—experience, would only be experientially real, within the context of the present moment in which we were experiencing it—we will always only ever be here now. If we honestly think about this for a moment, we will realize that the past and the future do not really exist, they are but fragments of memory (past) and projections of imagination (future), that are only ever appearing in the present moment.

The only time is now, and yet this is the last place our mind wants to settle. If we are not daydreaming about our past, most of us, most of the time, are worrying about our future. And yet, the elusive truth is that all we have is now.

The present is the one and only constant in life. It is the context within which the flow of life forms and transforms, appears and disappears. No matter what happens in our life, no matter what changes we may go through, we are always here, now. The moment is not an experience after which we must chase, it is the eternally pure and pregnant reality within which all existence unfolds.

We need to focus and train our awareness to be present in the eternal moment. Creation is a continuous act, an ever-unfolding process translating the infinite Divine no-thing-ness into the mul- titudinous reality of finite some-thing-ness. Every moment is a brand new creation, affording us the awesome ability to reboot our system at any moment. All we need is to become ecstatically aware of the infinite possibility contained within the seed of this very moment.

While contemplating conceptions of time and consciousness it is inevitable that one would encounter colloquialisms such as "be here now" or "live for today." Regarding these types of popular say- ings, it is important to point out the radical difference between living *in* the now and living *for* the now. To live *for* the now is to be limited by the moment. This may translate as being sponta- neous, but often the behaviors perpetuated in such a state, betray their blindly selfish origins and express little to no concern for their eventual outcomes. Living *for* the now is thus to live mindlessly, without compassionate awareness, or any sense of personal responsibility for anything other than the self.

To live *in* the now, on the other hand, is to mindfully behold the eternity of the present moment, that transcends and includes both past and future, including all causes and their effects. Living *in* the now is infinitely deeper than merely being aware of what is happening in the moment, that is just the content. It is being aware of the moment itself, which is the context that contains and connects all seemingly random phenomena occurring within its infinite borders. Events or experiences are the content of life, which occur within the empty space of the context—which is now.

The eternal present is an infinite openness that contains all finite expressions and experiences. Now-ness is a portal into all-inclusive awareness and aliveness.

To ground our awareness in the gift of the now, all we need to do is pause once in a while, to take a deep breath and become aware of what is; simply observe yourself and your surroundings. Then, to go even deeper, become aware of the space/time itself within which all that is happening occurs — this very moment. Think to yourself: It is always now, every moment. Whenever we feel distracted from the present - stop, pause, take a deep breath and return to the moment, which is truly all there is. It is never not now.

By design, the imagination has no sense of restriction in relation to actual reality; that is its strength as well as its weakness. Due to this dynamic, the imagination is capable of running wild and conjuring up all the worst possible scenarios that may or may not occur, overwhelming a person with fear about their future. But imagination is just that—fantastical, fluid, dream-like—it is not necessarily literal or concrete and, amazingly, when the actual future does arrive, it is often not nearly as bad as what one had so vividly imagined.

Simply put: Reality is hardly ever as bad as we feared it would be. A person with a good job or a person with a sick parent may think to himself: "If I lose my job or if my parent passes on, there is no way I will make it." As a result, their imagination runs rampant projecting all types of worst-case scenarios and crippling the person with fear. And yet, even if (Heaven forbid) you do lose your job or your parent does pass on to the next world, you will almost certainly survive and the reality, challenging or painful as it may be, will most likely not be as absolutely annihilating as your imagination had you believe. The point is this: it is a waste of time and energy to constantly worry about a future that may or may not materialize. It is much more productive to focus on being present in the moment, which is the only reality you are able to experience anyway.

Still, the question must be addressed: What do you do when the moment that you are experiencing is a painful one, one that you may very well want to avoid?

This is an ultimate existential question. Here is one potential response:

In life, no matter how difficult or painful a situation may be - whether it be a lost job, a broken relationship, or even the death of a loved one - if we truly wish to live in the liberating moment of now, we need to ask the right questions. The questions we ask of reality determine the answers we are able to receive; those answers then determine the shape and position of the window that we perceive our life through. We should not ask, "*Why* did this happen?" Nor should we try to explain a situation away like, "this happened *because* of x, y or z." These are diagnostic responses to experiences that look to the past for evidence of wrongdoing in order to place blame and explain the current condition of suffering. Rather, it would be much more productive to ask, "*What* could I possibly learn from this situation?" Or, to say that "this happened *for the sake of* x, y or z." These are future-oriented responses to suffering that seek to extract meaning and motivation from current conditions for future growth and development. In other words: whatever has already happened, has only occurred so that you can learn and grow in preparation for the next experience of now.

The question should not be *lamah* (Hebrew for "why"), but rather, *l'mah* (Hebrew for "towards what end"). When we ask 'why' our mind is focused on—and we are therefore stuck in—the past, searching for answers that never add up. On the other hand, when we focus on the potential trajectory of an experience or an event (l'mah), rather than trying to trace its genealogy (lamah), we resist the illusion of false certainty and remain open to the redemptive potential of the future by being fully present in the moment.

The truth is that we can never really know why things happen, at least on a theological level, since only the Creator knows every side of every story. But we can make a choice regarding what we will do next.

When we ask "why?"- we are looking to lay blame. When we ask "towards what end"- we are claiming responsibility for the co-creation of the new now.

Will we remain stuck in a predictable past of inevitable repetition, or will we choose to listen and learn and work to create a better future for ourselves?

The choice is yours.

□□

We can either control
or be controlled
by our circumstances.

When we choose to choose
we take responsibility
for our life.

CONTROLLING *or* BEING CONTROLLED BY CHALLENGES

□□

There are, essentially, two options when dealing with life's challenges: 1) We can view the situation as being, "above us," which means that it is transcendentally controlling us; or 2) we can view ourselves as being, "above the situation," with a bird's eye view. From that vantage point we have control over it.

To illustrate what it means to be either below or above a particular situation, picture this scenario: Imagine speaking with a friend who is having the same problem that you are currently experiencing. What would you suggest to them? It's always easier to see someone else's problem and to give them good advice than it is to diagnose and shift our own behavior. Why?

The difference is determined by whether you are experiencing the issue objectively or subjectively. This determines whether you are "above" the problem or "below" it. When it is someone else's problem, you are able to view the situation more objectively, as if you were "above" the issue.

When it is your own issue, you experience it subjectively, as you are immersed within it. The situation is therefore, "above you," controlling you from the top down.

Next time a challenge comes up and a decision needs to be made — whether it is a personal, business or spiritual issue — face the challenge, do not run away or procrastinate. But before you make a decision regarding how to respond, before you get pulled down further into your own subjective experience of the challenge, detach yourself for a moment and imagine a friend is asking you about this very same issue — dig deep inside, speak your heart to your friend, now follow that same advice yourself.

□□

Let's go a little deeper.

There is a part of us that struggles with imperfection and with not being 'enough.' Then there is a part of us that is always perfect and whole, lacking nothing and never feeling empty. One part is completely insatiable, always wanting more and more. When we have a hundred dollars, that part of us wants two hundred, and when we get that two hundred dollars, that part of us immediately wants four hundred. Simultaneously, there is a 'redeemed' and 'perfected' part of us that is always saying "*dayeinu*/enough, I am whole already."

Deep down, everyone knows what this means. The imperfect, desiring self, is constantly nagging us for attention. But the still small voice of inner perfection is also something we are inherently familiar with. We all have our moments, when we feel the most alive and the most real and true to ourselves, where life is not just about 'things,' objects, desires or wants. It is at these very moments that we are intimately connected with our soul, our inner perfection.

We are each comprised of an inner struggler (the imperfect self) and an inner *tzadik* (the perfect self). When faced with a challenge, we can either strive to do battle and overcome it or we can envision ourselves as standing above the situation and effortlessly master the issue with a calm and conscious response in the moment.

It goes without saying that it is mentally, emotionally as well as spiritually much more productive and healthy to see ourselves as whole, and to identify with our infinite portion of inner perfection, than to see ourselves as perpetually lacking and constantly strug-

THE POWER OF CHOICE

gling against the world and against ourselves.

To envision yourself as standing above your problem/challenge, you may want to use a little creative visualization, to imagine yourself as literally hovering above your circumstances. Visualize yourself as the most mature and evolved person in the world, effortlessly rising above your problems.

In addition to visualizations, you can also use verbal declarations to shift your perspective. For example, verbally declare to yourself that, "I really am a good person. There is a part of me that is truly free and above all of these problems. There is a part of me that knows exactly what is best for me; there is a part of me that knows exactly what I should do in this situation." Tap into that part of yourself, and move from there.

Imagine that powerful and perfect person is who you truly are ,and make choices based on the view from that perspective. When you lose your connection to this reality inside of you, stop, pause ,and take a moment to redirect your awareness towards your inner center of infinite perfection.

When you approach life from the perspective of your deepest, most perfect self, you will find that things which previously bothered you when you were in a narrow place of constricted consciousness, simply stop bothering you when you are able to access a more expansive awareness. You are no longer filled with anger, lust, jealousy or resentments. With one simple shift of perspective you are elevated above the minutiae of petty concerns. You suddenly realize that you are infinitely deeper and higher than all of these pesky problems and trivial pursuits.

This perspective is a choice you can make at every conscious moment. Are you going to invest in your highest, most perfect, and expansive self? Or are you going to choose not to choose, and live in a state of perpetual autopilot, viewing the world from the perspective of your smallest, most constricted, and imperfect self?

The choice is yours.

□□

The higher you climb
up the spiritual ladder,
the more expansive your vision should become.

If your heart does not soften
as your mind sharpens,
climb down and begin again.

Four Levels of Living

———

1 | Securing Physical Existence

2 | Loving and Being Loved

3 | Meaning and Purpose

4 | Feeling Connected

□□

In the course of our life's journey we have the opportunity to move through 'four stages' of personal development. These four stages are symbolically referred to as the four rungs of the ladder of our inner being. It is important to note that this metaphorical model is not one-dimensional or linear, leading from lowest to highest in a straight line. Rather, it is a veritable roller coaster of existential spiral dynamics that continuously loops back in on itself as one simultaneously progresses and regresses throughout the course of their spiritual and psychological development.

This image and process brings to mind Jacob's Ladder, from the Biblical book of *Beresheit*/Genesis, upon which countless angels were both ascending and descending from heaven to earth and back again. Additionally, each stage or rung contains every other stage or rung within it, in microcosm. This is similar to a set of Russian matryoshka dolls, in which each individual part, no matter how large or small, contains a complete set of dolls within it.

This teaching paints a moving picture of life as an infinite journey and perpetual path of becoming. And yet, so many of us seek some semblance of homeostasis and stability, rather than desiring to set out upon an endless alchemical quest of personal refinement and perfection. But the truth, and inner wisdom of life, is constantly calling us out beyond ourselves, beyond whatever we have achieved or established, out into the wilderness of the unknown where the real magic happens, and mystery awaits.

Generally speaking, most of us are content at whatever rung we are currently on, so long as we do not get a glimpse of the rung that is beyond us. If we are on rung one and are unaware of rung two, we will be satisfied remaining as we are on that first rung. However, it is also true that the higher one reaches, the deeper one experiences a profound inner happiness and sense of purpose. This dynamic, which rewards one commensurate to their level of psycho-spiritual development, creates a kind of magnetic pull towards greater complexity and maturation.

The real tension and struggle lies within the in-between stages (i.e. between rungs one and two, two and three, etc.), after we have lifted our 'foot' namely consciousness, off of one rung, but before we have planted ourselves firmly onto the next step. This is due to the liminal experience of having graduated from one level; yet not having fully settled into the next phase of the journey upward on the spiral staircase of conscious development.

□□

Let's delve a little deeper into this subject in order to explain it further.

These are the four rungs of the ladder in ascending order, which relate to the four levels of our soul:

Existential — *Securing Physical Needs*

Emotional — *Loving and Being Loved*

Intellectual — *Meaning and Purpose*

Spiritual — *Connection and Transformation*

EXISTENTIAL:
SECURING PHYSICAL NEEDS

At the first stage of growth, and we all begin this way, we are primarily 'existence' oriented. In the terminology of Kabbalah, this is called the level of *Nefesh*, which relates to our animating soul or vital life force. On that level, our entire pursuit is to ensure that our physical being continues to exist and flourish. Wherefore, we are primarily concerned with the basics of survival such as eating, sleeping and all action that is focused on our bodies remaining in good working order, ready for the journey of life ahead. Many people go through their entire life this way, just 'existing.' Even when they are older, their entire life is lived only on such a limited level of existence. They have careers, and maybe they are even successful, but they work long and hard hours, solely so they can continue to exist. They want to make money so that they can eat, they eat so that they can live, and they live so that they can work to make money to eat, ad infinitum.

People preoccupied with existence are more or less happy with their life. They work hard to put food on their table and keep a roof over their heads. Most people are content with this level of living. A person working to survive feels good and accomplished when he has enough resources to put food on the table.

Living primarily in 'existence reality' is fine in and of itself. The challenge emerges when one has secured his physical reality; he has amassed enough money, food and shelter to take care of his physical survival needs, both for himself and his family, and now he is beginning to feel called towards stage two. Once a person has the luxury of a secured existence, a new "vessel" is opened, a new need and desire is revealed. This is the beginning of the "emotional" stage of development, the second rung of the ladder.

□□

EMOTIONAL:
LOVING AND BEING LOVED

In this second stage, or rung, after one's 'existence' has already been secured, a person is no longer content with just working to make a living, to provide for himself and his family, on a purely physical level. Now he seeks emotional stability and mutuality. This is the innate human need to love and be loved, to appreciate and value another, and to be appreciated and valued by another. In the language of Kabbalah, this is the level of *Ruach*, which refers to the breath, or spirit, within. People on this level of development desire to feel the sensation of being alive, not just to survive physically. On a deeper level, they want to feel that they are loved and needed by someone who cares about them; and, even more, they want to show that same love to another in return.

Once we have begun to climb towards this second rung, no matter how secure our physical reality is, until we have secured our emotional stability we will continue to feel a lack in our life. One can have several million dollars in the bank and be totally financially secure, yet so long as that person does not feel loved and valued, and reciprocally, does not feel love for others in return, he will feel empty and discontent.

Once we are in a relationship or community and feel that we are contributing to the happiness of others that we hold especially dear, we have achieved the next level of happiness. But then, almost simultaneously upon achieving such stasis and satisfaction, a new "vessel" is opened and revealed. A new desire awakens for more meaning, clarity and purpose beyond our small circle of in-ter-dependents. This is the intellectual stage.

INTELLECTUAL:
MEANING AND PURPOSE

At this point, a person feels love and appreciation for and from others; yet now the person is no longer satisfied with only feeling and being emotionally secure. That inner need has been taken care of, as much as is possible, and now what one seeks is deeper meaning and purpose in their life. This entails developing a more intellectual understanding of the meaning and purpose of life in general, and of one's own life in particular. In the context of Kabbalah, this is the level of *Neshamah*, one's eternal and intellectual soul.

Some burning questions we may ask ourselves at this stage are: Why am I here? What is the meaning of my life? How can my life be lived with purpose and passion? For what was I created? What is my unique gift and calling?

Until these questions are addressed, explored and explained, allowing for answers to emerge, the person will again feel empty and lifeless. It is at such a point in one's development that philosophical questions take on a greater urgency. And yet, beyond the world of ideas and answers to such existential questions, there is the challenge of putting truth into action; this brings us to the realm of the spiritual, where practice, discipline and commitment to one's higher ideals becomes a top priority.

SPIRITUAL:
CONNECTION AND TRANSFORMATION.

At this stage, it is not enough for one to have a crystallized intellectual understanding of their life's purpose and inner meaning, they must live that purpose, they must act on those truths.

Once one has a good sense of their distinct path, a new "vessel" is opened and revealed, namely a yearning and longing to move beyond understanding in order to experience and express their unique individual purpose. In Kabbalah, this is the level of *Chaya*, the living or actualized self. This stage abandons linear development and requires a quantum leap of experience and awareness. There are many practices and techniques offered by the sages to achieve such a radical shift in one's entire being. *Further on in this text we will introduce a handful of such practices and perspectives. (For more in-depth study of these practical matters please see the many illustrative books on meditation and spiritual practice such as—*"Breathing and Quieting the Mind," "Visualization and Imagery," *and* "Reclaiming the Self"*).*

At this stage knowing our purpose is no longer enough. We want to live that purpose. Beyond knowing that we are infused with a divine purpose, we want to experience the Creator's presence in our lives, to truly live, feel and breathe our Divine purpose and meaning. This is the deepest level of life.

On this level, it is not enough to know that we are connected, we want to *feel* connected. We want to deepen and strengthen our connection with our highest selves, and with the essential truth of all reality, the Creator of all life. We want to live this connection, and better yet, to realize that we are always connected, as there is no real possibility of ever being disconnected; all is One.

One vital point to be cognizant of, when living through such a paradigm, is that each of these rungs/stages include all of the previous rungs/stages within them, but in a more expansive context. This means that the second rung — the emotional level — contains the first rung, the physical level; and that the third rung — the level of intellect — contains both the physical and emotional levels; the highest rung — the spiritual level — contains the physical, emotional and mental elements, all elevated to a higher, more refined and integrated level of experience. This means that moving from one rung to the next does not imply leaving the former level behind. Rather, as one achieves integrity on a particular rung they are meant to bring that integrity along with them into the next phase, not abandon the progress they have made on the previous level. For example: to achieve emotional well-being, one is not meant to ignore the needs of the body; they are now called upon to care for the body as well as for the heart. Each advancement requires that one take on a bit more responsibility for themselves and for others around them. Simply put, this is the psycho-spiritual process of maturation and manifestation.

Another similar, but subtly different, point to make clear is that each rung actually contains a subset of all four rungs within it. For example: there is the spiritual aspect of our physical being; this would be the highest level of the first rung. Similarly, there is the physical aspect of our spiritual Self; this would be the lowest level of the fourth rung. Essentially, the most refined stage of each rung is revealed when that capacity is consciously connected to the Creator. When one is able to sanctify a lower rung, it is only then that the next step presents itself.

We need to continually self-reflect and be honest about which level we are at. If, for example, we have been living from a place of Nefesh (basic survival living), and we now feel secure on that level, yet we are still experiencing a gnawing sense of dissatisfaction, we should understand that this is most likely because we are now in the liminal space between levels of being. Therefore, spinning our wheels faster and trying harder to survive and secure our physical existence will no longer bring us any more happiness than we have already attained. We need to be sensitive to the stirrings of our soul ,and step up to the next level, in order to seek and find a deeper and higher level of satisfaction.

It is towards this end that the remainder of the book is dedicated.

□□

IDENTITY

Every moment you are alive,
the Creator is saying:

"I need you!"

LIFE IS A BOOK

&

WE ARE ITS AUTHORS

□□

Moment to moment we are constantly writing and rewriting our own story, which is but a single chapter within the much larger story of humanity and of the world itself.

Each of our stories is radically different and can only be truthfully told by our most authentic self. Only when we live in alignment with our very specific personality, as well as our general "soul-type", will our spiritual, intellectual, emotional and physical uniqueness be fully actualized and expressed accurately.

Now let's try to understand this a little bit deeper.

In every experience of life, there is the experiencer, and there is that which is experienced. The 'experiencer-self' is that aspect of our consciousness that registers our experiences.

This is the aspect of our consciousness that can be referred to as, the 'witness-self' or the 'mirror-self.' This is the self that accompanies us through all of life's experiences, as it is not subject to change in terms of its form or function, only in degrees of subtlety and sharpness. This aspect of awareness represents the ability to be self-conscious at all.

This is the objective self, beneath the surface of your subjective ego personality. This is the inner self, through which your outer self comes into focus and being. Accordingly, this aspect of self is somewhat detached from your personal tastes and proclivities, as it is not limited or defined by that which you experience.

In addition to the inner 'experiencer-self,' there is the outer 'experienced-self.' This is the level of self that is effected and impacted by experiences, as they are refracted through the 'experiencer -self.' This level of subjective self is constructed from the content of your life, including your thoughts, speech, feelings and actions. The 'experienced-self' (i.e. the self that we experience as being our self), is the totality of every impression and experience ever encountered since conception. This self, changes and evolves throughout your life in response to specific experiences. The 'experiencer-self,' as mentioned, remains objective even in the midst of a subjective experience. The 'experienced-self'cannot help but be subjective, even in the most objective circumstances. In other words, the experienced self takes everything personally.

The 'experienced-self' can also be referred to as, your 'autobiographical-self,' or personality. This is the self that we all know—comprised of the particular ways that we think, feel, speak and interact with others. This is the self we are referring to when we say, "I know myself." What we are really saying is, "I know my story, my feelings, my thoughts, words and actions" (i.e., the content of my life).

This part of yourself, is in a constant state of flux, continually changing and evolving. When you are fifty years old and look at a picture of yourself from when you were five, this younger self looks and feels like a totally different person than who you are now at age fifty. And this sensation is partially true, at least in terms of how you look, feel and think as a result of all the accumulated thoughts, feelings and experiences you have gathered and internalized over the course of your life. And it is precisely these things which have created your 'autobiographical-self,' your personality. Through this lens, you really are a different person.

By contrast, the 'experiencer-self' is fixed and unchanging. It is, in fact, the very function of your consciousness that allows for the emergence of the 'experienced-self' in the first place. The experiencer self is therefore the necessary, often unconscious filter, which facilitates the creation of the 'experienced-self.' The general ignorance of this function is similar to the manner in which the lens of a camera is often taken for granted, in relation, to the content and imagery that is perceived through it. The 'experiencer-self,' the 'lens' of self-consciousness, is the context of awareness itself within which all of life's experiences are consciously experienced and interpreted. The 'experiencer-self' is the unchanging perspective that registers all the constantly shifting phenomena; it is the continuous conscience that observes the discontinuous lapses of reason; it is the uninfluenced soul that informs the influenced self; it is the observer of all that one observes.

SOUL-TYPE

Another name for the 'experiencer-self' is 'soul-type.'

No two people are alike by nature or by nurture—whether biologically, genetically, environmentally, culturally or spiritually—we are all utterly unique. We are each born with our particular 'soul-type.' This means that just as our subjective 'experienced-selves' are all different, our objective 'experiencer-selves' are also distinct from each other. This is similar to the way in which camera lenses are distinct from each other. They essentially all do the same thing, within the larger context of the camera as a whole, but some are bigger, some are sharper, some are shaped differently, etc. This means that we all enter the world with a particular perspective, even before we have actually experienced anything. Our 'soul-type' can thus be understood as the form of our lens, so to speak, or the shape of the mirror, upon which the details of our life story will be projected or reflected upon.

Another metaphor to understand this dynamic further; think of a blank sheet of paper (i.e. with no content). Yet, this blank sheet of paper comes in a particular shade, shape and texture. One sheet of paper is colored red and another is blue or green. One sheet of paper is in the shape of a square, while another is in the shape of a triangle or circle. The distinct coloring or shape of this paper is your 'soul-type,' that primordial part of you that never changes. What changes throughout life is what is written on the sheet, your personality, not the original shade or shape of the sheet itself - that is your soul-type.

The original coloring and shape of the sheet of paper, your 'soul-type,' is the composite of your natural inclinations, proclivities, talents and modus operandi. Even before we begin to write the first letter of our story, we are already distinct—possessing our own inborn tendencies and dispositions. One person is more inclined to be open and giving, while another is pre-disposed to being harsh and withdrawn. This is all a result of the particular coloring and shape of our paper, which in turn determines how each of our individual stories will unfold and be articulated, appreciated and understood. Of course we can all grow, learn and develop in new directions, but it is our 'soul-type' that determines the starting point of our life's journey.

Simply put, our 'soul-type' is the particular and innate way in which we think, speak and interact. Of course, throughout our life we pick up learned behaviors that modify these expressions of self, but here, we are referring to those patterns that are, in a sense, fixed or sealed within the very structure of our unique soul. These are the areas of our personal brilliance where we shine most brightly and feel most alive, where we are most distinctly ourselves.

Yet, we are also naturally predisposed to certain negative tendencies. These too are indicators of our 'soul-type' and hence, of our unique purpose and perspective. For example: some people are more prone to anger, while others may be more judgmental. Just as we need to pursue the areas and aspects of our greatness, we also need to exert effort to harness and redirect our innate negative tendencies. In fact, it is precisely these areas in our life, where we are most naturally deficient, that give rise to our greatest potentials, as we reveal previously dormant reservoirs of vast energy through the transformative process of rectifying our 'soul-type.'

To live fully and write our most authentic story we need to be in touch with the shape of our lens (i.e. our 'soul-type'), not just the content projected on the screen (i.e. our personality or accumulation of past experiences). We need to ensure that the story we are writing from day to day, and moment to moment, is consistent with who we truly are on the deepest level. We need to be absolutely sure that we are writing *our* story, and not merely living in the shadow of someone else's dreams, hopes, fears or fantasies.

The path towards self-actualization and fulfillment is founded upon the unearthing of, and alignment with, the infinite spark of the Divine; which is uniquely present within each of our personal finite lives.

The goal of life is not to lose our unique place within the universe, but rather, to find our deepest self within the overall structure of the cosmos, by living fully and openly from that place of authenticity. In order to accomplish this, we must first manifest our true individuality, which entails coming to an awareness of our specific purpose, enabling us to be more fully articulate in the moment.

Every person has his or her own unique purpose and mission. Generally, wealthier people must work on strengthening their attributes of kindness, openness and giving; while those less fortunate are often struggling to become more content with what they have and to not covet others' blessings. The magnitude of our souls' goals determines the challenges we will face, and therefore need to overcome, to achieve our true potential. From this perspective we can understand that even our challenges and 'lacks' are specially designed to help our soul grow in the way it needs to, in order to accomplish its mission. Accordingly, whenever we encounter these difficulties and challenges, we ought to keep in mind that everything, even our physical/genetic makeup, works in conjunction with the psychic/spiritual dynamics of our 'soul-type,' in order to assist us in achieving our unique purpose.

Essentially, everything in our life—both positives and negatives, privileges and challenges—is conspiring to help us articulate our unique story, at least as far as the tools that we need to succeed are concerned. Environment, culture, genetics, history—these are all ingredients that support and assist us in bringing forth our unique self in the best, most complete way possible. That does not mean the easiest, or most fun way, but the most necessary way for the good of your soul and the unfolding story of the world. Meaning that even when something or someone appears to be holding you back, they are really there to help you move forward, by forcing you to call upon your inner reserves, in order to rise above any challenge that they place before you. It is ultimately up to you. You cannot control what happens to you, you *can* control how you respond or react to it. It is your choice what you do with what you are given.

All the tools needed to achieve your maximum spiritual potential are apportioned in the measures that are appropriate for you. Both nature and nurture work in sync with your 'soul–type.' Every person has particular areas in their life in which they possess natural gifts. These are the things they love doing, even if, or despite them being challenging. Having a gift does not mean that it comes easy. It takes inspiration and a lot of perspiration to achieve your full potential. Still, in the great scheme of things, it is those very areas that we are soulfully connected with, and naturally drawn to, which focus our energy and awareness in the most productive directions to manifest our soul's purpose and perfection

And just as when we sense a powerful surge toward positively inclined actions we should pursue them, as this indicates that we are going with the flow of our soul-type, the converse is also true with regard to negatively inclined actions or desires. When we feel a powerful pull towards negativity, our work is to refrain from it; it is through this exercise of discipline that we strengthen our soul's connection to the positive. The areas in a person's life that contain their greatest faults or deficiencies, are the very places which hide the most awesome potential just waiting to be revealed. Whenever we feel pulled towards these negative behaviors or manners of conduct—be it lust, greed, laziness or anger—we ought to realize that these are precisely the areas we must pull ourselves away from ,in order to achieve our fullest potential.

The areas that we are naturally drawn towards and feel a strong connection with, positive or negative, indicate to us precisely where our potential can be made most manifest. When the attraction is positive we should follow it with all our heart, pursuing it and then pursuing it more. When the attraction is negative we ought to guard against it, and distance ourselves from it, with all the strength of our entire being. It is through acknowledging and engaging both our positive and negative attractions, in the appropriate ways, that we strengthen the core of our unique self and share the best version of our personal life-story.

□□

When what we Do
is rooted in Who we are,
we become aware that
we always Have
what we truly Need.

SENSE OF IDENTITY

———

From Being to Doing to Having

□□

*E*verything strives towards definition. In order to navigate, within a four-dimensional universe, we need boundaries. The same is true within our own selves. For better or worse, we are continually defining, and re-defining, our identity. As a result, we are always thinking about ourselves within a certain box or frame of reference.

The real question is: how do we, or how should we, define ourselves?

Broadly speaking, there are three types of people which is the three primary ways that people use to define themselves:

A. There are those who define themselves by what they *do*. For some people, being a professional (doctor, lawyer, artist, musician, investment banker, rabbi, therapist, computer tech specialist, etc.) is not only something they do or a polite way to introduce themselves to others, it is in fact a fundamental aspect of how they understand themselves; they define themselves as being whatever it is they are doing.

B. Then there are those who define themselves by what and how much they *have*. Not only do they project self-confidence, or a lack thereof, to the outside world based almost entirely on how much or how little is in their bank accounts, they even derive their own internal sense of self-worth from their material belongings. For such people, how much money they have, or how many cars they own, is the primary way they gauge their self-worth. They are truly, so they think, defined by what they have.

C. Finally there are those whose definition of self stems from *who* they are, their very *being*. For these people, their sense of self-definition is not based on what they have or even on what they do; instead, their sense of self is founded upon the rock of who they are at their core, beneath all the masks and trappings of the world.

These three dimensions—doing, having and being—are not contradictory, and they do not necessarily need to be in conflict. Every 'Who' should 'do' and 'have.' The only real question is: are we going up or down the ladder of growth? And, in which direction does one's self-definition flow? Does one's self-definition go from Being to Doing to Having, which is a positive trajectory? Or is it the reverse, from Having to Doing to Being?

Furthermore, what does this all mean and what does it have to do with living a happier and healthier life?

Sadly, most people's sense of self-worth and confidence, or lack thereof, is based on *what* they do and *how much* they have or do not have, instead of on *who* they are.

People tend to seek out and exert tremendous energy on attaining a career, their dream job. Often the definition of a dream job is one that offers a bigger paycheck at the end of the day; allowing them to have lots of things. Last on their list of priorities is discovering *who* they truly are so that they can achieve a deeper sense of wholeness and happiness, in order to live in alignment with their very being.

How does one untangle themselves from this predicament that is so commonplace in our society? One way to extricate yourself is to simply pause, breathe and take a few minutes to think deeply about your purpose:

"Why am I here?"

"Why was I born to my particular set of parents, with this specific set of genes?"

"What is my greatest asset and talent to share with the world?"

The simple act of asking such self-reflective questions can create a shift in consciousness from 'having' to 'doing' to 'being'—to 'being' to 'doing' to 'having.'

Rather than being preoccupied with what we do, or want to possess, we must first begin constructing our identity from the ground up, by discovering who we truly are, only then can we seriously consider what it is we are here to do. In this way, we can reverse the standard flow of society's self-definition and develop instead from 'being' to 'doing' to 'having'. Defining ourselves based on *who* we are, rather than on *what* we do or have, allows us to choose the rubrics by which our successes are measured. This is an essential step to reclaiming our autonomy, and access to deep and lasting happiness, especially in a society that bases so much of its self-worth on fleeting acquisitions such as material wealth and surface appearances.

When what we do with our lives is rooted in who we truly are, we will then authentically do what is right for ourselves at every moment. It is only then that we can become aware of the deepest level, where we always have what we need at any given moment.

◻◻

Argue on behalf of your greatness
and you will be great.

Convince yourself that
your success is impossible,
and it will be.

ARGUING ON BEHALF

OF YOUR GREATNESS

□□

We all have an image of ourselves—as well as of the world around us—that functions as a prism through which we observe and understand our lives. If this image is negative, you will feel deep down that you are unworthy, undeserving or doomed; therefore, you will continually fall short of your goals. If you think of yourself as worthless, you will indeed often act worthlessly.

In simple language—we become what we believe ourselves to be.

People who argue in favor of their own limitations, will get to hold on to them; as they live out these self-fulfilling prophecies and remain eternally limited by their own self-definitions.

Arguing for as well as defending your limitations will make you even more limited, perpetually downsizing your infinite soul, in order to fit it into the tiny box that you have built for yourself, forever becoming smaller and feeling more suffocated.

Sadly, this is true for many people. For whatever reason they feel they are underprivileged, undeserving, not properly educated, or born on the wrong side of the tracks. Unfortunately, because they believe that they have limited opportunities, they end up living this way, only to suffer the consequences of their own decisions.

That is not to say, that we are all born with the same opportunities at our disposal. Some people really are more privileged than others and are indeed born with a 'leg-up'; while others really do suffer from economic, physical, familial or societal challenges that impede their progress or mobility within the world as it is currently structured. We are not suggesting that these concrete realities do not exist, or that they should be simply, neatly and naively discarded. We are suggesting that these very real challenges—or obstacles—should not be seen as ultimately limiting—or defining of—one's soul potential. There are countless stories of people from all walks of life who have transcended their limitations or surroundings, enough to at least entertain the idea that we are all capable, on some level, of overcoming our individual obstacles. In fact, it has often been the case throughout history, that limited access to opportunities or resources has been a prime motivating factor for those who have successfully unlocked their limitless potential in a challenging situation.

With all this in mind, it is safe to say that a negative, or defeatist, self-assessment will—more than likely—put you two steps back from the rest of the pack. Before the race even begins, you're already behind. But the converse is also, and even more true. People who have a positive estimation of themselves, and a positive perspective on life, will generally be more successful, fulfilled and satisfied.

Beyond the idea that having a positive image of self and reality ,leads to a more positive, and productive life, we must understand that the more positive we are about ourselves and about life in general, no matter the circumstances, the more that positivity is attracted to us.

In a simple existential equation, we often get back in kind what we put out into the world. This may not be an immutable law of the universe, but it is experientially verifiable to a large degree, at least enough to seriously consider the ways in which our own actions and emotions impact our opportunities and obstacles.

If you believe deeply that you deserve goodness and blessing in your life, you will open yourself up to the light that is just waiting for the right vessel to receive it. Our self-perception and self-definition, impact the strength and openness of our 'vessel,' and as a result, dictate the quantity and quality of 'light' that enters our lives.

This is not some type of cheap superstitious pop-magic. This perspective is founded on an inherent trust in the Creator of all life, as it says in the Psalms, "one who trusts in the Creator will be surrounded by goodness" *(Psalms, 32:10)*. If you trust in the Creator of all life, the Source of all blessings, then blessings will surely flow in ways that are consistent with the quality of your vessel (i.e. your consciousness, capabilities or life context in general). At the very least, your ability to perceive previously hidden blessings will change substantially, allowing you to become more aware of the innumerable blessings that were, and are present, in your life.

Blessings attach themselves to those who feel themselves to be blessed, whereas "curses" most often gravitate towards those who feel themselves deserving of such negativity.

If you walk around thinking negative thoughts about yourself, or about life in general, then that is what you will see — more and more negativity. As a result, you will only reinforce your previously held negative perspectives, making yourself all the more susceptible to even more negativity coming your way. The cycle of negative thoughts, that in turn attract negative events, is often initiated by our subconscious as a way of proving to ourselves that "nothing good ever happens to me!"

But we have the power to break this seemingly endless cycle of self-defeat. Make the choice to see yourself as deserving and capable. Dare to transform your obstacles into opportunities. So often our truly limitless potential lies within the transcendence of our own limitations.

Argue on behalf of your greatness, argue that you can and will be great, by virtue of this, you will be.

Argue in defense of your smallness, convince yourself that your success is impossible, and that will be the result.

Life is best for each one of us, and indeed for everyone, when we each envision ourselves at our best, and live from that place of wholeness, inner strength and wellbeing.

Many things will stand in your way on the road to success, fulfillment and accomplishment. The least you can do is to make sure that one of those things is not you.

The choice is yours.

□□

The greatest gift
you can give another person
is to give them back
their self-confidence.

HEALTHY SELF-ESTEEM

□□

ealthy self-esteem demands a balance between self-confidence and humility. Unbridled self-confidence leads to arrogance and smugness, whereas, extreme humility can lead to disempowered feelings of unworthiness or of being incapable.

Self-confidence comes from the inborn awareness that we are inherently special and have something unique to contribute to our families, to our communities and to the world. Our existential uniqueness is a spiritual and biological fact. There is no one exactly like us, with our particular perspectives, experiences or abilities. Each one of us was created for a special purpose, to play a specific role, and to add our individual voice to the collective symphony. We can each take pride, and find confidence, in the fact of our own uniqueness.

THE POWER OF CHOICE

Humility emerges from the empathic awareness that everyone else is just as unique as we are. We are all in the presence of each other's ultimate uniqueness. Paradoxically, the awareness of our existential individuality is a shared universal experience.

Self-esteem then, comes from between these two properly balanced perspectives of confidence and humility.

Self-esteem allows you to feel safe and secure, even in the midst of a storm. This inner feeling of support, which buoys the psyche in turbulent seas, empowers you to dream big, work hard and to never give up hope even when the going gets tough. Self-esteem can make the difference between taking that necessary risk or playing it too safe to get ahead; between following your heart or settling for what's convenient; between landing that job or blowing another opportunity. As cliché as it may sound, the world responds to the external projection of your own self-reflection.

We may each access an even deeper degree of self–confidence, by tapping into our inner perfection, i.e. that special purity and holiness we all have deep within, on account of our unique 'soul-type.' On this level, humility emerges from recognizing that to truly grow and become who we are meant to be, we also need to confront and deal with our imperfections.

There is a dimension of self that is always pure, strong, true and noble (the soul). There is another dimension of self that is constantly struggling with internal as well as external obstacles, challenges, lacks and deficiencies (the ego). There is the perpetual struggler, and there is also the eternal tzadik/perfected one. Our personhood emerges from between these two aspects of self.

We are all unique. No two people are alike. In fact, we are not supposed to be. Each one of us is another distinctly beautiful gem, a specific sparkling of the Infinite Light of the Creator. To live fully and authentically we must strive to appreciate the fact that the Infinite One desires to be expressed in a multitude of finite vessels. Every person is a one-of-a-kind vessel, an exclusive expression of Infinity.

Never forget to be yourself. That is why the Creator created you.

□□

Confidence is recognizing
our own greatness;

Humility is recognizing
the greatness in others.

PRACTICE

Life can get heavy,
take yourself lightly.

LAUGHTER

□□

Tragedy is sad because it shatters form, and radically upsets our current comfortable reality, in a violent and intrusive manner. Comedy is joyous and inspires laughter, because it releases us from form altogether. It gently tampers with our perceptions, and allows us to transcend our rigid frame of mind and reference, in a playful way.

Laughter breaks us free from the freeze-frames of predictability and routine, opening us up, and softening our hearts, to see things from a different perspective.

The wise sage, Rav Simcha Bunim of Peshischa, was once crossing over a bridge when he noticed someone struggling below to stay above water. Unable to help the man himself, he shouted out to him, "Send my regards to the Leviathan" (the mythic giant fish of the ocean). The drowning man, struggling with his last bit of strength just to stay afloat, suddenly started to laugh at such an absurd request. He was then able to regain enough composure to grab hold of a nearby plank of wood, and thereby saved himself. Seeing the man as he emerged from the water, Rav Simcha Bunim explained to him that he was drowning because he was scared; and the more scared he became the more he lost control, and the more he lost control the more he panicked. He was therefore caught in a vicious cycle. His fear feeding his inability to think calmly in order to extricate himself from the situation. The perfectly timed joke broke through this pattern and released him from his fear; he was thus able to clear his mind and find the necessary tools and means at his disposal to save himself.

This is true of life in general. When people are especially stressed out, for whatever reason, they often do not notice the imminent opportunities close at hand, with which they can untangle themselves from their predicament. They get stuck. Fear grips them and they panic. Then, the more fear and panic they experience, the less they are able to see a solution to their problem. Ultimately, fear gives rise to more fear, slowly they lose their cool until they begin to feel as if they were drowning.

One way to untangle yourself from such a predicament is through laughter. Laughter makes us lighter and breaks the stranglehold of stress and tension, opening us up to see new possibilities, where before we saw only obstacles and despair.

Laugher takes us out of the rigid, defined, predictable reality and opens us up to more choices, options and possibilities than we were even aware of. The Hebrew word for laughter is *s'chok*. In Hebrew each letter of the Alphabet has a numerical value. The numerical value of the letters that comprise the word *s'chok*/laughter is 414, which is the same numerical value as the Kabbalistic term *ohr ein sof*/the infinite light. This *gematria*, (the Kabbalistic practice of numero-linguistic exegesis), suggests that through laughter we can rise above the world of form and routine, in order to connect to the infinite light, the Source of all blessings, the possibility of all possibilities. To illustrate this point even further, it is recorded that certain Jewish sages of old would start each lesson with a light joke in order to open their students' minds to novel information or new possibilities of deeper understanding.

The above stories characterize the quality and function of healthy laugher. Yet, a distinction should be made between healthy, productive laughter as opposed to cynical or superficial laughter. Outwardly they appear to be the same, yet there is a marked difference between the two.

Cynical, or superficial laughter, expresses the corrosive sentiment that life is meaningless and alienating. For example, people often laugh when they are frightened, uncomfortable, ashamed or just do not know how to react. This type of laughter is prompted by a sense of meaninglessness, or hopelessness and ultimately it only fosters more cynicism and even depression. Indeed, many professional comedians struggle with serious and sometimes crippling bouts of depression. In contrast, positive and productive laughter expresses a sense of release from limited perceptions of reality, with a recognition that everything paradoxically makes sense, albeit often ironically. When we respond to life with positive laughter, we can joyfully release ourselves from our limitations and stifled perceptions.

It is always positive to have a good laugh and take oneself lightly. It liberates and lightens us up. But we need to ensure that our laughter is positive and productive, not cynical or mocking. This is the difference between laughing *with* others and laughing *at* others.

We need to ask ourselves whether we are expanding and growing from our laughter; or, is our laughter sadly reinforcing a sense of meaninglessness and cynicism? Essentially, the question is: does your laugher depress or uplift you? Does your laughter confirm further uncertainty and cynicism, ultimately draining you of all desire to do anything? Or does your laugher shake you free from inhibiting form while opening you up to new possibilities?

Overall, we need to learn to introduce healthy, productive humor into our lives and work, especially in regard to ourselves, our loved ones, our families and our communities. Of course we need to be serious about our lives and about our responsibilities, but seriousness is often incorrectly translated as heaviness or even gloom. We need to be serious, not heavy.

As parents, for example, we have certain pre-conceived notions about our children and our homes, for better or for worse. The same is true concerning children and their parents. In order to have a happy and nurturing family environment we need to ensure that our home, the sacred space we create for ourselves and our loved ones, is permeated with a good dose of healthy humor. This allows each and every person to feel supported and free to be fully themselves.

With a little bit of humor, we can create a pleasant and happy home. When things do not go as planned—humor, tactfully and tastefully employed—can help to ease the stress of a challenging situation.

When tension does inevitably arise in the home, a little bit of humor can go a long way. In fact, sometimes it is the perfect antidote to dispel the toxic tension.

For instance, you can make your children feel safer, more loved and valued, just by adding a little humor when some type of strain arises between you. Maybe your child was careless and dropped an expensive plate, and you therefore need to gently guide them to be more careful; but why should what you say be heavy or humorless? To use another example, when you are trying to convey a particular message to your child, such as, that they need to take time to finish their homework, humor may help communicate this message without them feeling threatened or lectured.

This is also true in a situation where the tension is already present and palpable. For example, maybe your teenager is lashing out at you about how everything you do is wrong. Again, a response that includes a bit of good-natured humor will have a much better chance of diffusing the situation appropriately.

It goes without saying that this is also the case between spouses and in all interpersonal relationships. Even deeper, this holds true in regard to oneself. Sometimes we need to use a little self-directed humor in order to shake ourselves out of a stupor of anger or self-loathing.

Humor and laughter are effective tools that can be employed to diffuse a tense moment. However, to be effective, they must be used consciously and not carelessly. A misplaced joke or jibe can cause irreparable damage to a loved one's psyche or sense of security within the structure of a loving relationship. Laughter is powerful. Learn how and when to use it positively and productively. Never be too hard on yourself. After all, it is important to be able to lovingly laugh at our own mistakes, so that we can learn from them and grow as human beings without a crippling sense of guilt.

Patience is a virtue, but only to a point.

Wait patiently for the right moment
& when the opportunity
presents itself to do something positive,
do it right away.

ALACRITY

□□

*P*rocrastination kills every new opportunity. To procrastinate is to hold on to what was, instead of dealing with what is. When we procrastinate, we squander the present moment and all that it has to offer. This pro-active attitude is summed up nicely by Jewish sages of old, with the famous saying, "If not now, when?" And yet, doing things too quickly, or being in a hurried rush, is also not a positive or productive approach to getting things done. Ideally, one would be able to find a middle ground, between procrastination and hasty carelessness.

This virtue that is praised by the wise, is called in Hebrew *zerizus*/alacrity. We learn that this is a positive attribute from the Patriarch *Avraham*/Abraham, who rose early in the morning to perform the binding of *Yitzchak*/Isaac at the prophetic request of the Creator of the world. In response to this shocking request he did not procrastinate or push it off for later. He was told to take Yitzchak up to the mountain (which he assumed would be for the purpose of a ritual offering, although that was never the Divine intention) and he did so first thing the next morning.

Yet, as a careful reader may notice, Avraham did not set out to accomplish this task immediately when he was told, which would have been that very evening. Rather, he went to sleep and awoke early the next morning, refreshed and ready to meet this Divine challenge. He did not go at night because perhaps it would have been dangerous to travel in the dark; there may have been bandits or they could have gotten lost. Whatever the reason, he chose to wait for the morning sun. We learn from this narrative nuance, that doing things with alacrity does not mean being rash, robotic, impulsive or mindless. Rather, alacrity means doing things at the first opportunity that is available and preparing oneself appropriately in order to ensure, as much as anyone can, success.

Preparation is the key. The Jewish sages of old teach, *"zerizin makdimim l'mitzvos/*those who act with alacrity perform mitzvos (good deeds) early." That is the standard translation and understanding of this well-known rabbinic saying. But the actual wording in Hebrew is *l'mitzvos*, which means, "for the mitzvos," rather than the more grammatically correct word, *b'mitzvos*, which means, "in the Mitzvos." This teaches that those who are alacritous begin a task early by preparing for its successful completion. The doing of the task begins before the actual task is undertaken. Time to prepare, is therefore a vital component of successful performance in the completion of a task. In order to have time to properly prepare, one must begin earlier than he would have if he were to jump right in to doing something. This takes forethought, planning and alacrity.

Our challenge is to start tasks at the earliest possible opportunity, and to not push them off until later. If you can do something good right now or today - do it now, do it today. Do not think to yourself, "Ok, I will do it later, tomorrow or whenever I get around to it." When you think in such a manner you are: A) robbing yourself of an opportunity to do something positive in the present moment— which is all we really have; B) avoiding the present moment by remaining tied to the past, when this opportunity was not yet available; C) making an assumption that this same opportunity will be available tomorrow, when in fact, it is impossible to know such a thing with any degree of certainty.

As stated above, doing things right away does not mean rushing into them without preparation or mindfulness, rather, it means preparing yourself to accomplish something at the first opportune moment.

That being said, it is also important to point out that many people are prone to overthink, or even over-prepare for, a task. This dynamic is also not ideal. Yes, preparation is a key component of successful completion; yet one must be careful to not fall into the trap of over-analysis, which is often just a mask for fear or laziness. In such a situation it would be better for the person to just do it. Make a start, take a leap. If you fail or fall—that's fine—pick yourself up, learn from your mistakes and keep moving forward. If you want to write, write; if you want to learn, learn; if you want to work,

work. Just start doing something that moves you in the direction of your goal; perfection is not always the point. Usually, the process itself, which may very well include both successes and shortcomings, is the key to unlock the hidden purpose of our particular pursuits.

The best time to begin is always now: "If not now, when?"

□□

There is no excuse
to be in a bad mood around others.

Remember, your energy is contagious
and can either harm or heal
those around you.

JOY

□□

The Psalmist exhorts and inspires us to, "Serve the Creator with joy!" *(Psalms, 100:2)*. On a deeper level this implies that being joyous, in and of itself, is a valid and valuable way to serve the Creator. What is more, when we are joyful we are also serving ourselves and everyone around us as well.

Our energy is contagious. When we are happy we create a positive environment around ourselves. When we are feeling uplifted we have the power to elevate the spirits of everyone we come into contact with. Conversely, when people walk around in a gloomy, annoyed or depressed state, they bring down everyone else's energy with their own. Therefore, when we are joyful we are serving our Creator, ourselves and everyone around us.

Joy is infectious and transmittable. As such, it is a moral/social obligation to at least try to elevate our mood. We owe it to ourselves, and to the people we encounter not to pull them down; and

89

if we can, to even lift them up.

A person cannot think to himself, "So what if I am feeling sad or annoyed, who am I bothering? It's my problem not theirs." The truth is that it is not only your problem. Just by being in a bad mood you are impacting everyone around you. Your energy is contaminating and depressing those in your immediate vicinity. In addition to the benefit of your own wellbeing, consider how your mood affects other people; then try to think, breathe, meditate or visualize yourself into a better, happier mood.

The Hebrew word *b'simcha*/with happiness has the same letters as the Hebrew word for thought, *machshava*. We always have the ability to use our minds to consciously think ourselves into a happier state of being. Certainly, even if you are unhappy, you still have a choice to not walk around complaining about and bemoaning your life.

That is not to suggest that one should not discuss his problems or challenges with others, rather it is to emphasize that there are appropriate times when to share such things within the confines of loving, supportive, safe and receptive times and environments and people. It is up to us to consider others' willingness and ability to deal with our problems.

That being said, if you cannot think yourself into being more joyful on your own, take it a step further and try to act joyous (i.e.fake it 'till you make it); or better yet, surround yourself with people who bring out the best in you. Their energy will rub off on you as joy is contagious. It is up to us to do whatever we can to shake ourselves out of our depressed mood. Even when we cannot accomplish this fully, the least we can do is to not actively parade our sorrows before the rest of the world in some kind of masochistic—exhibitionist romp.

Of course, it is positive to deeply feel what comes up for you in any given experience, whether it be light and happy or dark and heavy. The trick is to not get stuck in any one emotional state, or confuse it for a static reality. All of our moods swing. Allow the waves of emotion to wash over, and move through you. Depression is often the result of confusing a temporary experience of negativity, for a permanent reality. Always know that the tides will change.

We are all aware of the power of "mind over matter," also known as the placebo effect, where the power of one's mind exerts a tangible influence over one's physical body. But the bio-psychic feedback loop works both ways. Meaning that we can also access and impact our mind or emotions through the actions of our physical body. Studies show that the physical act of smiling, even when you are in a bad mood, can actually shift your mental state. The movement of the muscles sends signals to the brain, which serve to disrupt the previously held patterns of negative thoughts and emotions.

This is all to say that you DO have a choice in the matter! The human organism is an instrument, which sometimes, needs a little adjustment in order to play in tune. Clearly, your environment and circumstances exert a strong influence upon your state of mind and health; yet we are not merely passive victims in this equation. You can either work from the inside-out (mind over matter) or from the outside-in (fake it till you make it). Either way, it's not a full-proof plan to never experience sadness or depression in response to the vicissitudes of life. But it is an empowering paradigm that allows you to feel like you at least have a vote or a hand on the wheel, so to speak. Take charge of your moods and the ways in which they impact your life. You cannot control everything, but you can attempt to shift the energetic scales in your (and everyone else's) favor.

DIVINE PROVIDENCE:

On one level, a lot of the sadness people suffer is because they lack direction. Depression often makes people feel that their lives lack cohesiveness, as if, they were just a random collection of unrelated moments. Joy, by contrast, is rooted and thrives within an overall awareness of purpose and direction.

Being truly joyful comes from the deep recognition that everything in life plays a meaningful role within a larger whole, even when we do not see it. Ultimately, this means that there are no such thing as an accident or happenstance.

When we do not experience any sense of order in our lives, we often fall prey to paralyzing feelings of anguish, frustration and laziness, which may lead to depression.

Being that our sense of inner joy is based on a rather intuitive awareness that everything is filled with purpose, coupled with the understanding that there are no coincidences nor accidents, a meditation on Divine Providence is in order. Maintaining a constant awareness of the spiritual trajectory within our own lives, allows us to use everything that happens to us as a Divine mirror; in which, we can (indirectly) perceive the Creator's guiding 'hand,' as it were, in this existential orchestration.

Begin by reflecting on your life, taking particular notice of how one thing inevitably leads to another. In the moment, when each individual event occurred everything seemed inconsequential, especially when perceived in a vacuum. Yet, when contemplated in retrospect and placed within a grander structure, the mandala of your life, it becomes crystal clear that each of these seemingly small events are intricately connected; and that when woven together as one they ultimately make up the multi-dimensional fractal pattern of *who* and *where* you are today.

Think about all the "big" things that you have experienced throughout your life, or even in the past year. Those are the milestones and peaks of your journey. Now pay particular attention to how it was often the small things, that simply happened in between those larger transitions and transformations, that created the possibility for those big things to happen in the first place. For instance, maybe you arrived late to a meeting, and because of that you met your spouse; or you just so happened to linger a bit longer at work than usual when you had face time with the boss and landed a promotion. These kinds of synchronistic examples are infinite, spinning out a seemingly endless web of cosmic collaboration between you, the Creator and the universe. If you are able to observe your life in such a calm and clear-headed manner, you will surely notice that many of the "big" things that you have in your life (your spouse, children, job and friends) are there because of the infinite array of seemingly small and random decisions you made in a moment.

There are no accidents and nothing is random; the more we realize and integrate this, the happier we will be. And, as mentioned previously, happiness is not only good for us—physically, mentally, emotionally and spiritually—it is in fact great for everyone.

RETURNING TO JOY:

On a deeper level—joy is who we are—it is our natural state. Humanity was born, as it were, in the primordial Garden of Eden, home of the Tree of Eternal Life and all earthly and spiritual delights. We are all inter- and intra-connected and thus we are naturally content and joyous, as joy ultimately comes from a sense of connection and purpose in our lives.

From this perspective, we do not even need to actively search for connection and direction to feel joyous – as joy is who we are at our root. It is our natural set and setting. When we find ourselves far removed from this reality we just need to find and hit our own personal reset button. This process of reset and return, to the pure state of being that most fully reflects who we truly are, ensures that we are able to regain access to the fruit of the Tree of Life, which holds the seeds of unencumbered and exuberant joy.

We all know that joy is our essence. When we suffer from emotional anxiety, stress or depression, these are merely concealments, or garments, that cover over and obscure our innate joy and inner light. The Hebrew word for depression is *atzvus*; the root of *atzvus* is *etzev*, which, when rearranged spells *tzeva*/color/paint. Feelings of depression can color or paint over the naked essence of our being, concealing the natural beauty of pure joy within.

We need to peel away the paint that conceals our natural beauty and release whatever negativity is weighing us down. We need to remove the paint to reveal our essence, which is pure joy.

Experientially, this process of erasing is an act of letting go. We need to let go of resentments and old grudges, whether these are negative feelings one harbors against oneself or against others, or even against the world. The more we are able to let go of these negative anchors, the more we allow ourselves to be carried by the constant flow of pure joy that is perpetually permeating the world and our lives. This river is always flowing, but if we do not channel it in our direction, our fields will forever lie fallow for lack of water. The more we let go of the negative past, the more we discover joy in the present.

Scanning the Body:

One more small point to keep in mind is that fatigue, or the state of the body in general, can also be a source of depression. This is related to the above conversation concerning our biopsychic feedback loop; how our mind can not only affect our body, but our body can also affect our mind, and in turn our emotions. Sometimes people feel sad, frustrated or confused, thinking that there is something wrong in their lives, when in truth all that is happening is that they are tired or hungry (low blood-sugar), or maybe they just ate a heavy meal and are feeling physically fatigued. People often misinterpret bodily sensations as emotional distress. When this occurs, it is a clear example of mistaking a sensation for a story.

Our innate need to make sense out of our lives demands that we explain—to ourselves at least—why we are sad or upset. As a result, we often grasp for answers or even concoct narratives to validate our embodied and inarticulate experience of being tired or hungry.

In the midst of such an experience, as we seek to rationally explain our irrational feelings of anxiety and alienation, we look for a hook to hang our feelings on, rather than admit that we just need a nap or a snack. And in those heightened moments, our stories feel so real. In fact, we might actually touch upon or uncover some deep-seated psychic or relational truth in the process, but we must not confuse these stories with the sensations that we are experiencing.

Sometimes stories and circumstances can produce sensations, but it can work the other way around as well; sometimes sensations spin out stories to explain why we are feeling what we are feeling. For this reason, it is best not to think too deeply about your life (i.e. where your life is headed or how your relationships or jobs are going) while you are tired or hungry, such as right before bed or if you have not eaten for a significant amount of time. If you feel yourself starting to slip into a state of anxiety or panic about your life, try to pause for a moment and take stock of your body. Ask yourself, "Am I tired? Am I hungry? When was the last time I ate?"

If you feel like you are losing your mental bearings and emotional balance, try tending to your body first before embarking on any serious existential considerations. Contemplating your life and any big moves or necessary changes is often more successful and satisfying when approached from a settled, calm and relaxed state of mind. When you are tired or hungry, everything feels worse than it really is.

□□

Equanimity liberates us from
the desperate need for others
to accept or validate us
and allows us to just be who we truly are.

Never allow others people's opinions about you
- whether positive or negative -
to affect you

EQUANIMITY

□□

*P*eople assume that their thoughts, feelings, words and actions are the calculated result of their own choices. They function as if in a vacuum, unaware of the input and influence from the outside world. As a result, they firmly believe that their decisions and desires are wholly their own. Sadly, and to be quite frank, most people are merely a collection of the impressions that others have made upon them. They are a little bit of everyone they have ever met, but not in a good way. They are the sum total of all the traits, some positive and some not so much, that they have picked up from the people they have encountered throughout their life.

For instance: Someone (seemingly powerful or important) at some point (an especially vulnerable or impressionable moment) once told them a certain story or idea, and ever since then they just so happen to think this way, without ever really challenging it. Or, maybe there was a situation in which a person that they respected showed very little compassion towards a homeless person on the street, and ever since then they have internalized this behavior as well. We too may notice that a person particularly close to us may have said or done something that we uncritically accepted and integrated into our own behavior or worldview. At the end of the day, we are the sum total of all the people we have ever met, especially those we have admired or feared. These extreme cases exemplify a passive and unconscious approach to the art of life-craft and the process of becoming one's own person.

On the extreme end of the spectrum, there are some people who are so deeply effected by others that they base their entire sense of self-worth and value on second-hand observations and outside-opinions. Their inner-self is completely dictated by outer impressions. They let the world tell them who they are supposed to be.

There are those who are aware of this tendency. They therefore carefully choose to surround themselves with people that elevate and nourish them with positivity.

Of course, social norms and life circumstances do not always allow people to choose where they are and with whom they interact. You may need to interact with a nasty bank-teller or ask for a drink from an unfriendly flight attendant; you may even find yourself living in an oppressive or dysfunctional family or community situation.

One common approach to dealing with negative influences is to construct and secure a defensive mental-wall, or barrier, to protect yourself within an impenetrable suit of 'character armor.' Doing so allows you to go wherever you wish, for even if you find yourself surrounded by negativity or negative people, you have already erected a wall of protection to maintain your existential equilibrium.

This option may help you be impervious to other people's negative energy, but it can also place a barrier between you and the people you encounter, inevitably creating a kind of disconnect. As a result, you end up feeling aloof and separated from life and from other people. Clearly, in certain situations this ability to disconnect from one's immediate surroundings or influences is much needed, and as such, it is a good practice-technique to develop and use when needed. But what we are ultimately looking for is a way to be protected from negative outside influences, without shutting ourselves off entirely from the world and life.

A subtler approach is what is called in Hebrew, *hishtavus* or "equanimity." This practice allows one to maintain his individuality and composure throughout all of life's situations, while at the same time, remaining open and engaged with other people and with the world.

Here's how it works: equanimity is the inner sense that life is as it should be; no matter what, it is always perfect and whole. Whether people praise or scorn you, or, for that matter whether you are eating foods which you relish or foods which you dislike, it is all completely equal to you. Not that you become stoic in the face of life or indifferent to other people—a compliment is still a compliment and tasty foods are still tasty—but these things just do not matter enough to be able to throw you off kilter. You remain rooted, in a deeper foundation that allows you to maintain a state of emotional equilibrium, even in the midst of life's ups and downs.

To illustrate this point, here is a recorded anecdote:

Rabbi Yitzchak/Isaac of Acco, the great 13th century Kabbalist, tells a story about a student who once approached a spiritual master and asked him to teach him the secret wisdom. The teacher, in classic fashion, responded to this request with a question of his own. He asked him: "Have you attained equanimity?" The student was thrown off guard and asked the master for clarification as to the meaning of this very specific question. "Well," replied the master, "do you feel happy when you are praised or sad when you are derided?" The student responded: "Yes, master. I do feel good when I am complimented and I do feel bad when I am criticized." The teacher then immediately dismissed him on the spot and told him to come back when he had achieved equanimity.

Equanimity liberates us from the endless cycle of relentless desire and its inevitable consequence—suffering. This is the meaning behind the statement of the rabbis of old; "He who wants to live, let him die." This short, paradoxical rabbinic teaching conveys the ultimate futility of pursuing a path of permanent satisfaction or satiation. By its very design, life will inevitably disappoint one fixated upon a particular outcome. The sooner one lets go of expectations and attachments to a desired outcome, the sooner one can actually achieve some semblance of emotional equilibrium. This is the idea of being *in* the world, but not *of* it.

When we learn to master the art of equanimity through meditation, we find ourselves less affected by other people's energy, while still remaining open and available in the moment of immediate encounter. In fact, one might argue that equanimity, although rendering one unaffected, may actually allow one to be *more* present with other people. This can be seen clearly, as one's emotionally-charged reactions and self-validating perceptions, tend to obscure the light of others with whom one is interacting. The simple awareness of equanimity gives rise to a more refined level of connection and compassion (i.e. once we remove our ego from the interpersonal encounter) in order to receive the other in a more open and welcoming manner.

To practice and develop this state of equanimity, begin by taking a few moments every day (preferably in the morning) for objective introspection, asking yourself the following questions:

1) Do I need other people's praise to feel good about myself?

2) Without praise, do I feel less significant or special?

3) From where do I gain my sense of self-worth?

4) How do I feel about my life when not comparing it to others' expectations or achievements?

You can also add a creative visualization by imagining yourself doing something praiseworthy, such as helping an older person carry groceries home or helping someone less fortunate get back on their feet in a substantial way. While entertaining an image of yourself at your finest moment, ask yourself: "Am I looking to see if someone else is observing me? When no one is looking at me, how do I feel about doing this noble act? Do I secretly wish that someone else would see me? Or does this not matter to me whatsoever?"

By asking these pointed questions, you may come to the devastating realization that your sense of self-worth is completely dependent upon other peoples' observations and opinions about you.

But all is not lost, as knowing the problem is half the solution. The mere recognition of the fact that you care so much about what others think about you, will itself allow you to begin to care less.

The truth is that what other people think about you, or the energy (especially negative) they project towards you, is not your problem, rather its their problem. We can only control, and we should only seek to control, issues that are "our problem." What other people think about us, or the energy they project toward us, is something *they* need to deal with. It is therefore "their problem." Something that is beyond our control. We ought not confuse the two. We need to work on our own issues and leave others to work on theirs.

Spending time thinking about and clarifying which challenges are truly yours, and which are, in reality, someone else's, empowers you to actively focus on those things that you can actually change.

This will simultaneously allow you to accept, and let go of, those things that are ultimately outside of your control.

When we focus on our own 'stuff,' we build ourselves up from the inside and start to secure a solid sense of self. A side effect of this new found strength is that nothing another person says, feels or thinks about you can have any real or substantial effect on your own state of mind and sense of self; this is the foundation of equanimity.

□□

Expect nothing.

Appreciate everything.

GRATITUDE *IN* EVERY SITUATION

□□

L ife presents us with many different opportunities, challenges and experiences; some we interpret as good and some we perceive as bad. Yet, the feeling and attitude of *gratitude* should be a constant.

Being grateful does not mean that you have to be grateful *for* every situation you encounter, rather it implies be grateful *in* every situation. The ultimate goal is to realize that whatever the situation may be—it was meant to be, and thus we are grateful that we are alive to experience it, whatever it may be.

(Admittedly, this is a difficult perspective to maintain, especially in more painful or traumatic experiences. Nevertheless, it is a beneficial mind-state to cultivate, hard as it may be to achieve.)

Once we are grateful *in* every situation and realize that whatever happens to us is for the benefit of our spiritual growth, we will acquire the ability to realize that everything which occurs in life is our teacher.

Cultivating gratitude in all situations, also allows us to develop the ability to overcome any sense of dissatisfaction we may experience, in regards to whatever life has put on our plate. All of life's experiences are part of a balanced diet that can be digested and metabolized for the nourishment of our soul's purpose. There are no 'throw-away' experiences, everything can be ingested, recycled or composted; there is energy and value in all of life's experiences— whether positive or negative.

We live in a disposable age, where everything in our lives seems to be expendable, from the cars we lease to the plastic cups we drink from. Sadly, this sense of disposability extends into our private lives and relationships as well. If we are always looking for the newest product or the most cutting edge gadget, then why would we stop with objects? Why not extend this approach of instant gratification and unending novelty to all aspects of life, including our love-lives?

Many people have indeed applied this disposable consumerist mentality to partnership and marriage. As a result, the divorce rates around the Western world are staggering.

The truth is that this sense of insatiability and existential dissatisfaction can never be filled with things or mere novelty. In fact, the more we attempt to fill our lives with material possessions or novelty, the emptier we feel; that is because every time we fulfill a desire, our vessels of desire expand. And as the vessel expands, so does the feeling of need and dissatisfaction. It constantly takes more and more ad infitum, in an attmept to satisfy the growing emptiness within our soul.

Rather than always seeking out the next best thing to satisfy your existential emptiness, you should be able to transform what you do have, into what you need.

If you are able to cultivate a mindset of gratitude for what you have, you will realize that you already have everything you need.

The bottom line is this: Without gratitude you feel empty so that even what you do have, you really don't. Being grateful fills your heart and lifts your spirit so that even what you don't have, you really do.

The choice is yours. Choose gratitude.

□□

The greatest gift
we can give ourselves
is to give to others.

GIVING BY RECEIVING

□□

People tend to believe that the more they receive, the greater their pleasure. And yet, the opposite is true. In fact, the most satisfying pleasure in the world is not to receive, but to give.

The greatest gift we can give ourselves is to give to others. A person experiences more inner joy, and lasting pleasure, from giving than from receiving. Think about this for a moment. When you walk down the street and drop a coin into a needy person's cup, don't you feel better than if you had found that same coin for yourself?

Simply put: We receive by giving.

The Biblical Hebrew root word for 'giving,' is *natan*. The Hebrew letters that make up the word *natan* are *Nun*–(N), *Tav*–(T), *Nun*–(N); a palindrome, (meaning that the word can be read both forwards and backwards), N-T-N. This is an allusion to the idea that when you give to another, you actually get something back yourself. You give and get in return, with one action.

The deeper reason for this phenomenon is that by giving we are accessing our deepest selves and tapping into the spark of the Creator, the Ultimate Giver of Life, which is within us. By giving, we are transcending our limited role as creation and entering into the infinite realm of the Creator.

Being open and responsive to the needs of another can be expressed within the context of three general paradigms of giving and receiving:

1) The ME paradigm

2) The YOU paradigm

3) The WE paradigm

Let's explore these three a bit deeper:

1) In the *me* paradigm there is a me and there is a you, I am doing you a kindness by giving to you. I am aware of a distinct me, as separate from, a distinct and independent you. I am showing *you* love out of the goodness of *my* heart because I want to. It is all about me, and I have all the power.

2) In the *you* paradigm the act of charity or giving is not about the *me* at all, only about *you*, the other. This can be expressed in the

context of love as one lover losing him/herself within the wants and desires of the other. One loves the other to the extent that he/she forgets about him/herself. It is all about *you*. You therefore have all the power.

3) In the *we* paradigm both me and you are creative expressions of the One Creator. Therefore, we are essentially one. It is not about me or you, but rather about *us*. What is good for me is good for you and vice versa. In this sense, we both share power.

The *me* paradigm is a biological and natural state. To love and look out for one's self is as natural as breathing. It is what motivates us to eat, sleep, procreate and keep ourselves out of harm's way. Self-preservation is innate and healthy. At its most extreme, it can be totally self-centered and abusive as everything and everyone are related to as mere objects, or experiences, to be used for one's own benefit and pleasure. The *me* paradigm is where independence is established.

The *you* paradigm is an emotional state. On the most basic level, it is what inspires us to connect with others; to compromise for the sake of a relationship. It is what makes friendships, families, collaborations and communities possible. At its most extreme, it leads to the shadow side of love, in which, one person completely sublimates their own needs, desires and selfhood to the desires and demands of another. The *you* paradigm is where co-dependence is acknowledged.

The *we* paradigm is a spiritual state, in which, each person/part recognizes their integral role within the greater relationship/whole. To love another human being as yourself is to understand, on the deepest level, that the other person and you are essentially one. As you are both parts of a larger whole, the health and wellbeing of each one of you is dependent upon the wellbeing of the other. It is on this level that we realize, there is a collective *we*. We are all limbs of one cosmic body, we are all branches on the Tree of Life. The *we* paradigm is the realm where inter-dependence blossoms.

Healthy self-love stems from the knowledge that our lives have intrinsic meaning. We are each vested with a divine purpose. We all matter. We all have something unique to contribute to our own personal self-development, as well as to the perfecting of the entire world. The *we* paradigm is founded on the recognition that, just as I am special and unique and have a specific soul-purpose, so do you.

For interpersonal or romantic relationships to be successful, and sustainable, *we* need an awareness that both *you* and *me* are in it together. The relationship is greater than the sum of its parts. *We* are creating something together that transcends each of us alone. This gives birth to the recognition that, for a relationship to grow, there needs to be two involved parties—a fully realized and expressive *me* and a fully present and responsive *you*—and that ultimately *we* are creating a relationship together as *one*.

□□

PERSPECTIVE

Desire more
because you are inspired,
not because you feel
like you have to.

KNOWING WHEN TO PURSUE

OR REJECT

A STRONG DESIRE

□□

Desire is the engine of life. We all have desires – that is human nature.

*E*ach desire indicates to us that there is an emptiness or lack that needs to be filled. It simultaneously alerts us to the fact that there is some type of energetic soul-connection between us and that which we desire—whether person, place or thing.

A desire can either be a creator of connection or a destroyer of integrity. Desire lights a fire. Sometimes fire warms and catalyzes, other times fire burns and consumes.

There are desires that we need to pursue, as they are generative and life affirming; and there are desires which we need to resist, as they are exploitative and detrimental to our overall wellbeing. Desires reveal the energetic bond between us and that which we desire; such energy can either be released through fruition or through friction. Sometimes energy is released by engagement, suggesting a harmonious and positively collaborative energetic relationship. Other times energy is discharged through abstention, indicating a dissonant or potentially destructive relationship between the desirer and the desired.

Sometimes we need to pursue a particular desire, and it is through such engagement that we will achieve our energetic elevation. But other times the healthy option is one of avoidance. Either way, the divine sparks within what is desired are released if interacted with appropriately (i.e. engaged when it is positive, and avoided when it is negative).

The question remains: how do we know which desires fuel life and should be pursued, and which desires destroy our integrity and should be abstained from?

Honest self-reflection would be the simplest answer. When a particular desire arises, ask yourself: "Is this desire good for me physically, mentally, emotionally and spiritually? Or will it be bad for me on some or even all of these levels? Is obtaining the object of my desire going to advance my emotional/mental/spiritual development or is it going to hinder my growth? Will the satisfaction of this desire put me two steps forward or two steps back from where I want to be?"

Admittedly, this is an over simplification. Most of the time we are too subjective and invested in our own satisfaction to honestly admit if a particular desire is good for us or not. This is especially true in the moment of active desire, when we are prone to rationalize almost anything to get what we want. In such moments, we must be especially on guard against impulses and urges that trigger deceptively enticing internal monologues to persuade us into misguided actions. These are the veritable lobbyists of desire — making pitches, offering bribes, or threatening actions if their demands are not met.

One interesting exercise you can do (when you are not in the midst of hunger, passion or anticipation of the fulfillment of a particular desire), attempt to make a list of your most common and familiar desires and honestly assess each one in terms of it being healthy or unhealthy. Of course, this list could be even more detailed and situational than a series of black and white blanket statements. In fact, the more detailed and situational the list is, the more accurately you will be able to deconstruct the multiple ingredients and impacts of a particular desire.

One part of establishing a more conscious and self-controlled response to desire is to learn to untangle ourselves from the subjectivity of the moment, then respond with expanded awareness from a more objective and clear-headed space. How do we do this? How can we make an objective assessment of our most private desires? By stripping away any sense of perceived pleasure we think we would receive from the fulfillment of this particular desire.

One way to temporarily separate yourself from the anticipated personal pleasure, is to imagine that you are giving advice to another person regarding the very same issue.

For example, let's say you are having a strong desire to change jobs. Instead of thinking only about yourself and clumsily attempting to determine what exactly is the root of this desire and whether pursuing it will positively advance you or not—imagine that you are speaking with a close friend about the same exact situation and that they are asking you for advice. What would you tell them from an objective point of view (i.e. when the pleasure of fulfillment or pain of abstention is not your immediate experiential concern)? How does the situation look different from a bird's eye view? Does it all add up, or are there unforeseen blind-spots and previously unconsidered pot-holes?

Now that you have no personal investment in the desire other than the overall wellbeing of your friend, what would you tell that other person to do? Would you tell them to pursue or refrain from this desire? Whatever you would tell that other person to do, take your own advice and do that.

□□

Life can either be
a random collection of disjointed events
or a unified whole
that is constantly meaningful and
continually connected
— the choice is yours.

A LOT *VS.* EVERYTHING

⊡⊡

here is the paradigm of "a lot," in which we feel there is a large number of things going on in our lives (job, family, social responsibilities, physical health, mental well-being, spiritual development, etc.); and then there is the paradigm of "everything," in which we feel there is an overarching umbrella-like theme to our lives and all of the individual details are contained within that context.

Our life is either a collection of randomly disjointed experiences, ideas, feelings and sensations; or, it is a unified whole that includes multiple experiences, ideas, feelings and sensations. Depending on which paradigm we are living from, we will either feel scattered and unfocused while being pulled in different directions; or, we will feel focused and connected as one.

In the Biblical narrative when *Yaakov*/Jacob encounters his brother *Esav*/Esau after years of conflict and separation, each brother speaks to the other about his own life. Esau says in Hebrew, "*yesh li rav*/I have a lot;" whereas Jacob says, "*yesh li kol*/I have everything." On the surface these two statements seem quite

THE POWER OF CHOICE

similar, but when contemplated deeper they are radically different.

There is a profound difference between thinking in terms of "a lot" versus thinking in terms of "everything." Besides the obvious, which is that a person can have a lot and not have everything (even when a lot is everything one needs), there is a distinct difference between relating to life from the perspective of "a lot" in contrast to the perspective of "everything."

These are not merely quantitative statements. On a deeper level, they reflect one's perceived quality-of-life as well. Having "a lot" does not only mean that you have a lot of things, it implies that whatever you do have feels like "a lot," meaning a lot of individual, disjointed things. "Everything," on the other hand, is a unified perspective. This is a "big picture" vision where all the things in your life are inter-connected within the context of the whole.

We live in a culture that tends to think in terms of *a lot*. When viewing one's life as a whole, one often thinks, "I *have* a good relationship with my parents, with my spouse, with my children; I *have* a nice home or apartment, a car, an iPad or iPhone; I *have* a job; I *have* my hobbies and friends; I *have* x amount of money in the bank, etc." This is a life full of stuff. With nothing connecting the dots, it just seems like a lot of disjointed elements coming together to fill empty space. There is no harmony, or greater pattern, it is just, "an endless sky full of stars with no constellations." This is, as it says at the very beginning of the *Torah* account of creation, there was a state of *tohu v'vohu*/chaos and void that existed before any light, order, awareness or articulation entered into the creative process of world-formation. Which is essentially what we are talking about, just on a more personal, micro-cosmic level.

Beyond the lack of focus, and general feeling of random confusion that occurs in the paradigm of a lot, there is also the absence of a sense of ultimate satisfaction. For there is always a newer phone, gadget, product, car, partner or experience on the market. Today you have one thing, tomorrow you want another.

For example: Someone buys a new iPhone or a new pair of shoes and this causes the person to get really excited. They feel so elated after their purchase, that they decide to call a friend, to tell them the wonderful news of their latest acquisition. But after a short period of time, maybe even as they get off the phone, the nagging restless emptiness resurfaces, once again they are on the lookout for the next new and exciting thing to fill the hole in their heart.

In the paradigm of *a lot* there is total fragmentation; there is one thing, then a second thing, and then a third. There is always a sense of needing to catch (fill) up because there is no intrinsic wholeness.

From an *everything* perspective there is a whole-system understanding of life, in which all things are contained and connected within the greater context, that is larger than the sum of its parts.

The ancient rabbis teach that, "There are empty people who are filled with positive deeds as the seeds of a pomegranate." On the surface this statement is paradoxical. Why are such people called "empty," when in fact the end of the statement specifically says that they are filled with as many good deeds as the (numerous) seeds of a pomegranate?

Similar to the seeds of a pomegranate that has each one encased within its own individual shell, which separates it from the others, the good deeds of such "empty" people are fragmented and not connected to each other within the structure of a greater whole. These are people that may do a good deed today, and perhaps another one the next day, without any sense of cohesion, meaning or harmony connecting their actions or life choices within a holistic framework. The good deeds are wonderful acts and should be valued as such. However these people remain empty at their core, as there is no overarching theme of goodness to focus their actions in a desired direction or conscious trajectory, which provides life with a sense of purpose (something that is essential to connecting the dots of one's seemingly isolated experiences and actions).

To build a spiritual and sustainable life of wholeness, unity and harmony founded upon an *everything* paradigm, we need to secure a big picture vision for ourselves. The way to do this is by uncovering our deepest purpose. Why are we here? What is our divine mission? Why were we born at this period of time, in this environment, to this set of parents, with these siblings, genetics and cultural influences?

When we think deeply about our innate uniqueness and natural talents, we must seek to determine how we can offer our particular gift(s) to the world in a manner and medium that is positive, productive, powerful and profoundly impactful. Think about your natural talents, proclivities, tendencies, strengths and challenges. Ask yourself: What are the things I do that make me feel the most alive and connected? What passions and pursuits bring meaning and fulfillment to my life and to others'? Once you have determined what your gifts are (including why and how you want to develop, pursue and offer them), it is up to you to channel and direct them in ways that articulate your highest spiritual, mental, emotional and physical potential for the betterment of yourself and the world around you.

When we uncover (and recover) our purpose (and passion) in life, it becomes our *everything* paradigm — the unifying and underlying structural principle that inspires, includes and elevates all the details of our life within a grander scope.

When we live a life of *everything* instead of a life of *a lot of things* our approach is from a place of integral inclusivity. Each and every detail of our existence plays its own role in the greater picture that is our life. It is not this thing here or that thing there vying for our attention. It is not a struggle between being a good parent or person *vs.* being successful in a career. Each aspect of our lives becomes a detail that contributes to the wholeness of our overall purpose in the world. This creates a feeling of expansiveness and harmony, rather than dichotomy and strife.

□□

Learn to read the signs the
universe is showing you
in order to know whether
the world is
supporting or resisting
your decision.

CERTAINLY UNCERTAIN

OR

UNCERTAINLY CERTAIN?

□□

I n an earlier chapter we discussed two different approaches to determining whether a particular desire is worth pursuing, or if it is better left alone. The first approach is to become aware of the subtle internal sensations and motivations that arise when you are considering whether or not to pursue a certain course of action. For this approach to be effective, you need to develop a refined sense of sensitivity and self-awareness in order to discern whether you feel contracted, constrained and constricted, or expansive, alive and elevated in the face of a particular desire. It is through gauging your own reactions or taking your own temperature, so to speak, that you are able to evaluate a given situation. The second approach is to assess your desire objectively by imagining that you are counseling a friend in the same situation. This approach requires a degree of detachment and compassion in order to yield positive results.

In addition to these two approaches, there is another set of in-dicators that can help to determine if a particular desire is worth pursuing or if it is better left alone. This is the approach of trying to read the signs that the Creator is showing you—via the uni-verse—in order to discern whether the world at large is supporting or resisting your decision.

Practically, this means that when you are making a decision—such as, whether or not to buy a particular home or enter into a specific relationship with another person, for example—it is wise, once that decision has been reached, for one to pause and ask one-self: Are things going smoothly? Are there bumps in the road? Is the world supporting me to purchase this home or to go deeper into this relationship? Or is it the opposite? Sometimes you make a decision to do or buy something, or to be with someone, and right away numerous obstacles and hardships set in; it becomes a labor intensive experience. It seems as if the world is telling you, "stop, don't do it, let go."

Broadly speaking, there are "certainties" and "uncertainties" in life. Let us take the example of wanting to purchase a home. If, logically it "makes sense" for you to buy the home (i.e. you have the funds put aside, it is a buyer's market, you need to live near that area because of schools, family, community, etc.), then ignore the hardships that arise. They are mere obstacles that arise in your path meant to test your mettle and sharpen your resolve. No matter what comes up and no matter how hard the process becomes, pur-sue your dream of buying the home. Even if it only happens with great difficulty and challenge, do not say, "well, if it was meant to be, it would be easier." In such a scenario, where your desire makes sense and fits in with your larger life-picture, to say such a thing would be a copout and a form of self-sabotage. With regards to the "certainties" of your life (i.e. you must purchase a home in a certain area, for instance), do *not* let the "uncertainties" that emerge dissuade you from your goal or dream. When there is certainty in your mind, heart and soul, persevere and patiently push forward, do not pay attention to the external obstacles and uncertainties.

Then there are times when, in truth, you are actually uncertain about a potential course of action. There is no overwhelmingly logical, emotional or even spiritual pull to pursue a particular home or relationship, and yet, it seems so natural and easy. Everything around you seems to want to help you move forward towards this particular purchase or relationship. Yet you are not one hundred percent convinced, either mentally (it does not make logical sense to buy this home or enter into that relationship), emotionally (you do not have a gut feeling that this person is right for you), or even spiritually (you do not feel a deep soul connection to this home or person), it just all fell into your lap and seems to be going so smooth and easy. In this case, when there is "uncertainty" in your mind, heart or soul, it is best to use the "certainty" of the world around you, to guide you towards what is right and good for you. If, once you make the decision to pursue the home or the relationship, everything continues to go easy, then by all means move forward. This is the way the Creator—using the creation—is showing you that you are on the correct path.

If, however, it all starts off easily and smoothly, but the moment you pursue the object or person further there arise setbacks and hardships, walk away. The "certainty" of the universe within the context of your own internal "uncertainty" is showing you what to do.

In summary:

When you are certain about something, do not let the uncertainty of the world sway you from your path. Stay the course and overcome all obstacles.

However, when you are uncertain about something, attune yourself to the certainty of the Universe, allowing It to guide you on your journey.

□□

When you are comfortable
with yourself,
wherever you are,
you are always at home.

EXILE & FREEDOM:

———

DISPLACEMENT *or* ROOTEDNESS

SILENCE *or* SPEAKING UP

FORGETTING *or* REMEMBERING

BEING INFLUENCED *or* BEING THE INFLUENCER

□□

The human desire for freedom is innate and universal. The concept of freedom is both intuitively simple and existentially complex. For our purposes here, let's just say that freedom is the opposite of exile, which ultimately leads to slavery. (In essence, exile is the root of slavery.)

Exile can be both external and internal. Physical or political exile is when a person or a people are uprooted from their homeland, environment or family. Most times such exiles are externally imposed — one or one's people are forcefully driven from their native environment into a strange and unfamiliar habitat. But there can also be internal or existential exile, where one feels isolated and estranged from his or her deepest self. In fact, internal exile can be even more devastating and challenging than external exile. One can be free in a jail cell, while another can be in exile within the walls of their own home.

To be in exile means that we are disconnected from the ground of our being.

To be free means that we are empowered to express ourselves in a manner that is true to our experience.

Let's explore the dynamics of how one descends into a state of internal exile.

□

There are four steps that make up the descent into inner exile and existential enslavement:

1. The process of alienation begins when a person does not feel comfortable where they are. They feel out of place, like they do not belong there.

2. Because they feel out of place they silence their true voice and refrain from expressing themselves.

3. In doing so, they feel even more uncomfortable and lose their dignity and natural balance; they 'forget' who they are and become disconnected from how they truly feel.

4. As a result, they assume the persona that others expect from them, and start acting like others around them, just to fit in.

These four stages can be observed in simple social settings. Say for example, you are at an event and you do not feel comfortable being there. You feel a bit out of your element and you don't know the other people there very well, or they are too smart or too silly for your taste, and so you silence your voice in order to "fit in." Slowly you forget your true identity, and before you know it, you have put on a mask to become somebody other than yourself. Oftentimes we are not even aware this is happening in the moment. It takes real sensitivity to attune ourselves to our inner voice and true motivations. Developing the characteristics of transparency and honesty is a necessary first step towards existential freedom.

The Biblical book of Exodus speaks of the people of Israel descending into bondage and eventually being redeemed as a free people. A closer look at the text reveals these four levels as outlined above. The book begins with Jacob and his entire household leaving Israel to go down into Egypt. In the beginning of the book of Exodus each member of Jacob's household is listed by name, meaning that each member of the family had their own established identity. As their exile intensifies, the text drops their names and refers to them with impersonal pronouns. The unique and specific individuals become a non-descript and general "they," as in, "they multiplied, they increased" *(Exodus, 1:7)*. Not only do they no longer have names, they lose their voice as well. Even in the midst of slavery, we do not hear them articulating their experience or voicing their opposition to such oppression.

The first step of the Israelites' exile was that they were misplaced, literally and figuratively, from their homeland and native environment. The next step was losing their names and voices. In other words, they lost their ability to express their inner truth.

Feeling lost and silenced by their surroundings, they began to forget who they truly were and from where they came. Their *da'as*, the Hebrew word for "awareness," was in exile. The knowledge of their true identity was obscured, hidden and lost. Once they lost their grounding, of true self, their core identity was eroded (or concealed), and they became totally open to being influenced by outside forces, views and voices. This dynamic led them to becoming existential and ideological slaves.

The definition of enslavement is when one is controlled by external entities or energies which are not rooted within one's indigenous self. A slave is someone whose life is completely fused with, and dependent upon, his master in such a way that he has no identity of his own. A person lives as a slave so long as he is uncritically influenced and persuaded by outside voices that are not consistent with his own true nature. This compels him to behave in ways that conform to the expectations or measurements of another. In such a situation a person has, in effect, surrendered his uniqueness to his surroundings. This is a form of slavery.

Nowadays, we are all in danger of becoming slaves to advertisements, politicians, educators, parents, friends, the internet and any other external voices that are not our own. One must be vigilant in his efforts to maintain his inner essence in the midst of such rampant manipulation on the part of the market, the media, pop culture and even his own community. Being able to hear the still small voice amidst the raging storm of competing agendas is no easy task. It requires conscious commitment, compassion and creativity.

So one more time, the descending stages of exile are as follows:

First, you feel (or are) misplaced. You are out of your personal comfort zone and feel that you do not belong. Because of this you stay quiet and shut yourself down, silencing your own voice. As a result, you forget your true identity and become uncritically open to outside influences until, ultimately, you begin acting in conformity to your surroundings, even against your will.

The first step into personal exile is the most dangerous, because it is a slippery slope from there. Once you feel out of place—intimidated and shut down—before you know, it you have forgotten who you are, what you stand for and what you believe in. It is then only a matter of time before you begin acting like others just to fit in. Clearly, sometimes the best course of action in a challenging situation is to be quiet or receptive, not because you are forced to, but rather because it is the wisest thing to do in a particular setting. But here, we are talking about something altogether different. In the context of exile, we are referring to a feeling of externally imposed self-silencing, an uncomfortable situation in which one feels that their voice would not only be misunderstood, but would actually be forcefully silenced or discredited should they attempt to speak out. Sadly, for some people this is not only a once in a while scenario, but a way of life.

There are some people who are merely reflections, or clones, of others around them. As mentioned, such individuals are a mere accumulation of all the impressions and expectations of everyone they have ever met, particularly those whom they deemed important. They are "slaves" to everything they hear and see in their immediate environment or in the media. They are constantly and continuously influenced and shaped by outside stimuli without their free choice or consent.

When a person lives this way he or she is a slave to surroundings. As a result, that person ends up living out someone else's ideas and identity instead of their own. (Because there is a total eclipse and occlusion of self-identity, one starts living as the other.) A secondary, superimposed reality supplants their true-inner-identity, until eventually, all that is left is a reflection of other peoples' ideas and impressions of them.

❑

To break this pattern of unconsciously reactive behavior you need to remember 4 basic truths:

1. You always belong, no matter who or where you are. Wherever you are, that is where you belong. Nothing is accidental or random and you have a right to be wherever you are. The fact that you are in a certain place at a certain time is because there is a Divinely orchestrated purpose for you to be there. There is something special that only you can achieve by being in that exact place and time; a lesson to be learned—or taught—or perhaps, a good deed to be done. You should never feel "out of place."

2. You always have the power, and right, to express your opinions. You should never feel forced to silence your voice, although sometimes you may choose to do so. In less comfort-

able situations it is always wise to consider in which manner it would be best to express certain opinions, if at all. However, this should never be dictated by someone else. Never let anyone take away your voice against your will.

3. The one thing no person can ever take away from you is *you*, your Self, your identity. Never forget who you are and what you believe in, and stand for, at your core.

4. If you find yourself in a negative environment, make sure (if possible) that you are the influencer. Be aware and cautious not to be influenced by any negative elements. Uphold your integrity, even in the midst of opposition.

It can be a fine line between exile and freedom. Oftentimes it is up to us to decide which state we will live in. One can be free in prison or exiled at home; the choice is within. Exercise your freedom, so you don't lose yourself in exile.

□□

SHEDDING
THE NEGATIVE

There is the physical sensation of anger,
and there is the story behind the anger.

When we learn to separate the
sensation from the story,
we release ourselves from
the toxic cycle of negativity.

DEALING WITH ANGER

□□

*E*motions, in and of themselves, are neutral. It is how we express them, that makes them either positive or negative. Our ability to courageously feel, and fearlessly articulate our emotions, is a sign of maturity. The power of choice arises in the space between feeling and expressing. This is not to promote a paradigm that is devoid of emotional expression. Quite the opposite, in fact, all people are capable of developing themselves to the point that they can process and express their feelings in a positive way.

Anger, like all emotions, can be used for positive or negative purposes. Positive anger can motivate us to stand up for what we believe and to speak truth to power regarding injustices or inequalities in our families, communities or society at large. Negative anger, on the other hand, can send us spiraling out of control, often in ways that harm others closest to us.

We all know that anger, if expressed unconsciously, can be detrimental. Acting unconsciously out of anger is harmful to ourselves and others. Anger can make a person do, say or think things that they would never condone under normal circumstances, things which they almost always regret. And yet, so many people struggle with anger.

If we retroactively reflect upon our own behavior during times when we were possessed by anger, we will most likely come to the conclusion that it did not do anyone, ourselves included, any good. Then why do we keep getting angry? To help us take control of our pre-programmed patterns of anger, and to more consciously harness our emotions, we need to get to the root of this all-too-common issue of unconsciouAnger is rooted in that fragile part of our ego that lives in a perpetual state of fear. Fear of what?—you may ask. That is different for every person. It is not any *one* fear that leads to anger, it is the *mechanism* of 'ego-rooted fear' itself, which harbors and breeds our feelings of anger. This fear can be healthy at times, as it protects us and our ego from outside attack or dissolution. However this fear can also take on a negative charge, when we become too attached to maintaining our egos at the expense of either growing beyond ourselves or connecting to others in a vulnerable and authentic way.

For the most part, anger thrives within a self-centered paradigm. This is predicated on the idea that we know exactly how life ought to be and how events should unfold. For instance, you are driving carefully down the highway and a car comes out of nowhere and cuts you off—do you immediately and reactively flare up in anger? Why? Because, on a most basic level you think that this was not supposed to happen to you, since you are such a careful driver. When things do not work out the way you thought they should, you become angry.

ANGER & IDOLATRY:

Underlying the emotion of anger is the ideology of idolatry. In the act of becoming angry we are declaring; "The Creator's light has become manifest to me in the car that just cut me off, but I reject it. I know better and I have another idea of how things should be."

Of course, the person who just cut you off did so of his own volition (exercise of free choice), so, from the perspective of the present moment, events did not necessarily have to occur as they did. This leaves the door open for you, to become angry that events did not unfold differently in the moment, as well as, to ignore the potential lesson or opportunity for personal growth introduced by this particular series of events; as your externally directed anger overwhelms your ability to be self-reflective. And yet, from the perspective of the past, as something that has already happened, it is most helpful to see the occurrence as something that was essentially "meant to be." From this vantage point you can try to accept the fact that you needed this experience in order to learn or do something positive. By rejecting it, and becoming angry in response to the situation, you are effectively saying that life is just a random series of various events. My ego and perception of reality were tampered with by this other person. The Creator has nothing to do with this particular instance. I am angry.

Three Approaches:
DOING, WRITING, VISUALIZING

Regardless of everything we know about anger, and how anger is rooted in our smallest, most constricted self, information alone does not always translate into practical behavioral change. There is often a divide between what we know and how we act. This is the essential difference between the Biblical Tree of Life and the Tree of Knowledge. The Tree of Knowledge tricks us into thinking that knowing something is enough. Once we think that we know something, we become self-satisfied to the point where we don't even put what we have learned into practice, which is ultimately the end-goal of all spiritual teaching (i.e. putting truth into practice). The Tree of Life refers to what is known as "walking your talk"; the Tree of Knowledge is all talk, so to speak.

For instance; let's say a person learns all about anger, they read hundreds of books about the negativity of anger, they go to week-long seminars focused on overcoming anger, they know that anger not only hurts the people around them, most often their closest loved ones, but that it also hurts them as well. And yet, often, when they are provoked or challenged they still flare up in uncontrollable anger. It is not that they choose to become angry. It is more like the knee-jerk reaction of an unconscious emotion that seems to be rooted within the deepest strata of their psyche.

What can be done in such a situation? How can we transform our deeper selves, so that even our unconscious reactions and expressions are positive and not blindly violent or hurtful?

One approach is the path of doing; as it is through consistent and repetitive actions that new, consciously chosen, behaviors are able to become second nature. It is through the practice of right action, rather than just right intention, that we can transform ourselves on the deepest levels. This can be a highly effective technique to alter our behavioral patterns from the outside-in, so to speak.

The goal is to train ourselves to have new, positively charged, responses to situations that previously elicited our anger. Conscious actions, when performed regularly over time, eventually rewire the brain to respond differently, even when it is responding on a subconscious or instinctual level. For example, the next time you feel your anger building, take a walk, a deep breath or count to ten. When we do this over and over again it becomes second nature. But it takes work. Over time, and with training, your body will automatically respond to a stressful situation by taking a deep breath or counting to ten to regain composure.

Another path to healing your anger is to write a letter detailing all of your negative feelings towards the person who has angered you; then read it to yourself imagining that person, sitting right there in front of you, listening intently. Do this for an extended period of time, forty days in a row is recommended, as forty is symbolic of transformation, and see what happens. Your anger may dissipate, you may gain a new dimension of clarity around the situation, you may develop a higher degree of compassion for the other person, you may even tire your anger out, and in the process you will be liberated from its emotional stranglehold. This can allow you to move on from the situation in your own way, or to gain the necessary composure to address the issue with the other person in a different and more mature manner, bringing closure, by simply getting your ego/anger out of the way.

A third approach to dealing with your anger, which sidesteps your logical linear left-brain and impacts your deeper subconscious psyche, is through various forms of visualization and guided-imagery. In general, it is very effective to bind any abstract ideal that you are striving towards to a resonant image that represents the attainment of that goal; and further, to vividly visualize yourself achieving that goal.

The visualization itself can either be positive or negative, depending on your internal make-up and what you generally respond to. For instance, you can visualize the negative effects and impact of your anger. Try to conjure up an image of yourself the last time you burst out in anger, how silly and overly-dramatic you acted, how hurtful it must have been to others around you, how toxic and embarrassed you felt afterwards. Alternatively, you can visualize the positive effects of *not* acting out of anger. Imagine yourself in a challenging situation while retaining total emotional control and compassion. For most people the positively charged visualization has a more wholesome feeling to it, but there are many people who respond more to the shock and embarrassment of the negative imagery. This is for you to decide, it requires honesty and self-awareness.

Keep in mind that for a visualization practice to be effective, you need to imagine the scene as precisely as possible. Do not spare any of the details, elaborate on them as much as possible, down to the minutia of the imagery. If you are visualizing yourself in a peaceful room controlling your anger, take notice of the colors, the patterns and the texture of the walls. Literally see the color of the shirt you are wearing. What do the other peoples' clothes look like?

If you find that you have a hard time conjuring up these images, you can use your other senses to help support the visualization process. For example, imagine over-hearing a bystander's conversation that is occurring while you are flaring up in anger, "wow, that person has no control over himself;" or, "I thought he was such a nice person, I can't believe that he speaks to people that way." In this way, if you are unable to actually 'see' the image on its own, the audio imagination can help to stimulate the visual dimension in order to create a fuller picture of the experience.

SEPARATING THE STORY FROM THE SENSATION:

One important point that needs to be understood is that everything previously said about the negativity of anger is only referring to the "narrative" of anger, the storyline attached to the sensation itself. The story behind the anger, and its interpretation, is what is (usually) negative. The sensation of the anger itself is generally neutral, and can be harnessed and even steered in a positive direction.

To explain:

There is the sensation of anger, (adrenaline rushing, flushed cheeks, heightened blood pressure, etc.), and then there is the story behind that anger (i.e. "she said this;" "he didn't do that;" "it's not fair"). Let's say that someone does something to you that you consider a violation. For example, you are an artist and someone tells you that your art is no good. You become angry and your heart starts racing. There are two things happening here: 1) there is the physical sensation in your body, the visceral reaction of your heart racing, your palms sweating, your cheeks flushing; and 2) there is the mental narrative in your mind, fueling the anger towards the other person. True, the anger in the body is triggered by the story in your head, yet without the story to back it up, it is simply a sensation like any other. It is neither positive nor negative. In fact, the visceral feelings associated with anger are essentially the same physical responses to any kind of excitement or passionate anticipation.

As soon as we subscribe to a particular story and connect it with the narrative behind the anger, we are caught in a trap. The anger becomes our master and we lose our ability to freely choose how we wish to respond with clarity and compassion. Our responses are therefore knee-jerk and reactive, based on ego and fear. Even when there are righteous causes for positively charged anger and indignation, such as social or moral injustices, we run the risk of over-identifying with these narratives and losing touch with the physical sensations within our body. With the anger in charge, we react and lash out, not necessarily in the most productive manner.

When we are mastered by an angry narrative, our sensational responses are unconscious and fear based.

How can we overcome this 'story' and escape such a trap? One way to deal with anger is to separate the sensation from the story. This way it is no longer "my" anger caused by this person or that series of events, rather, it is reduced to the neutral physical sensation of anger. One is then able to utilize the raw energy of the sensation itself, and direct it towards a productive act (i.e. taking a run around the block, doing a positive deed with zest, or working to right a wrong in a way that will actually yield results rather than just discharging your own out-of-control emotions). This repurposing of the sensation of anger for positive outcomes, not only improves the quality of one's life, but the lives of others around him as well. In this process, the ego is channeled away from a purely self-centered existence and put in service of a more joyful life.

It is often the story behind the sensation that;

A. inspired the sensation of anger in the first place, and

B. prolongs the sensation itself by validating your "right" to be angry and to treat another person poorly.

Sensations pass, as any experienced meditator will attest; stories, on the other hand, persevere through time and space, as any anthropologist or psychologist will agree. Once activated, they will each continue generating the other, spinning the wheel of anger and emotional outburst ad infinitum, unless they are separated and seen for what they really are. A story does not have any pre-ordained interpretation or response. And in fact, sometimes a response other than anger will yield healthier and more productive results in tough situations. Similarly, not every sensation requires a complex mythology, or conspiracy theory behind it, to validate your experience of it. Sometimes a sensation is just a sensation. We do not always need to find a reason why we are experiencing a particular feeling; it is not always someone else's fault or responsibility.

Sometimes a sensation is just that, end of story.

But how do we mentally separate these two, disconnecting the sensation of anger from the story behind it?

In every experience there is that which is experienced (the feeling) and there is the experiencer (the feeler). When we experience a feeling, there is the "I" that is experiencing it, but the "I" is not the experience or the feeling itself.

In simple words; you are not angry, you are experiencing a moment of anger.

The experiencer is fluid and dynamic; whereas the actual experience is defined and static. Do not allow your emotions to define you. Emotions are something you feel, not something you are. You are more than any one emotion at any one moment. You are the limitless capacity to experience all emotion, you are the consciousness that can contextualize emotion within a grander structure, you are the cosmic creative impulse incarnate!

When anger is triggered and wells up in your body, another way to diffuse the situation is to pause for a moment and allow yourself to feel the sensation of anger in the moment, without connecting it to the story that seeks to rationalize your "right" to be angry. You can observe yourself as the sensations of anger move through you, all the while not becoming attached to or identified with those sensations, just observing them and allowing them to dissipate. You can say to yourself; "look at me feeling angry. I can feel it in my body. I am really triggered." Eventually, the sensations will subside. If you are able to patiently wait it out, without reacting while in the midst of a sensation, you will have successfully navigated the stormy sea of your internal emotions without getting stuck on the rocks of your self-righteous narrative.

The goal is not to not become stoic, indifferent or stone-like, where nothing ever affects you. Rather, by simply pausing and observing yourself experiencing the sensations of your anger, you are seeking to cultivate a mind-state where you can truly feel them for what they are. Simultaneously, you are also letting go of the storyline behind these sensations. This is a way for you to be fully present "in" your emotions, without ever losing yourself and "becoming them."

The more you are able to separate your sensations from the stories that produce them, the more you will have the power to choose your life and create your own thoughtful responses.

□□

The illusion that we
have full control over every situation is
the root of much of our anxiety.

There is a Controller,
but it is not you or I alone,
rather,
it is the Master of the Universe.

LEARNING TO LET GO

□□

*L*ife is a continuous cycle, a constant flow of energy and experience from life to death and from death to life.

At a sub-cellular level, the elements that make up who we are (our atoms, quarks and gluons) are perpetually being annihilated and recreated, almost simultaneously dying and being reborn. Our skin, for instance, is renewed every month; our stomach lining every four days; and the surface cells of our intestines every five minutes.

This rhythm and cycle is also reflected in our breath. We inhale, exhale, and then inhale again. Inhaling is an act of filling ourselves, enlivening our bodies, a "life moment." Exhaling is an act of emptying ourselves, escaping our bodies, a "death moment."

THE POWER OF CHOICE

In this way, we see the patterns of life manifesting on multiple levels at once. Truly, as both ancient mystics and modern scientists have discovered and keep re-discovering—the microcosm is a reflection of the macrocosm. Cosmically speaking, the flow of the Creator's energy into this world is similar to the cycle of our breath. The Creator's 'exhale,' fills all of creation with life, energy and vitality. And then immediately, almost simultaneously, so as to allow finite reality to remain in existence, the breath of life returns to the Creator in a Divine 'inhale,' which is mirrored in creation's 'exhale.' The flow of life thus moves constantly back and forth, exhaling and inhaling, running and returning to and from the Creator, into and out of creation.

This process is not only constant and continuous, it is also relational and collaborative. In the same way that humans and trees are part of one eco-human life-cycle of carbon and oxygen, Creator and creation are also re-cycling the breath of life. The Creator's exhale is creation's inhale and creation's exhale is the Creator's inhale. Every moment there is a cosmic exhale into the world creating, forming, animating and sustaining creation anew at all times, as well as a simultaneous and immediate returning of that life force, a cosmic inhale.

Our own microcosmic inhale is a welcoming of new life and vitality from the flow of the Creator's energy that is exhaled into creation; our exhalation is the returning of that life-force back into the universe and into the Creator's inhale.

From our perspective, the inhale represents our ambition to live and succeed, it expresses our innate desire to attain more, to fill ourselves with life and new experience. The exhale is our serenity and surrender, the space in which we let go of all striving and seeking, it expresses our submission to everything being just the way it is in the moment.

For life to be lived to its fullest, it must include within it the element of 'death,' represented by the exhale. We need to learn how to live well, but just as importantly, we also need to learn how to die. This means being comfortable with taking a break from yearning and ambition in order to simply let go and just be.

Life is best lived proactively. We need to work hard and be fully engaged, involved and ambitious. And yet, at every moment, we must simultaneously cultivate a strong awareness that our lives are in the hands of the Creator, and with every breath we are returning/exhaling all of our life energy back into the Source of all Life. This awareness leads to the realization that everything we have in our lives is truly a gift from Above.

□

To live as a human being is to grow, to move forward, to expand and evolve on every level—physically, financially, mentally, emotionally and certainly spiritually. Our happiness is dependent upon our ability to change and grow. *Sameach*, the Hebrew word meaning "happiness," is closely related and phonetically connected to the Hebrew word for "growth," *tzomeach* (the S is exchanged with the Tz; this is an ancient Kabbalistic exegetical technique of substituting letters with similar sounds and properties to arrive at hidden and novel meanings, as well as relationships between words and concepts).

Despite the discomfort that often accompanies a growth spurt, we are happiest when we are in the process of moving towards some meaningful goal. When we are thus engaged, we are being true to the nature and rhythm of life, since all of creation is in constant flux and transformation, even something as seemingly still as a mountain. And yet, while this quality of constant striving and growth is essential to the human condition, the need to let go and understand that ultimately it is all in the hands of our Creator, is equally essential to our success in life on many different levels.

The ability to let go is as crucial to our ability to grow and succeed, as is our desire to strive and attain; they are both part of one cycle. One is always in need of the other in order to maintain balance in both stillness and motion. We must learn (to allow ourselves), to take a physical, emotional and mental break from all of our activities; and to deeply know how this too, is a part of the rhythm and cycle of life. In this way, we come to understand and appreciate the role of cessation within the process of creation. This is the message of Shabbat, the seventh day of creation, when the Creator completed the creative process by ceasing from activity. This rest was not considered "after-the-fact" of creation, it was in fact the final phase of the process.

We need to take in, to hold on, to inhale, and also to give up, to let go, to exhale. Just as naturally as we take things in, from food to attention to money and property, in order to be a fully functioning part of the whole-system flow of life, we need to know when and how to let go and to give up, to relinquish our claim and possession. This movement is a swinging pendulum between attachment and non-attachment, between doing and being, between holding and, when necessary, letting go of all our preconceived notions and expectations in order to simply move on.

Living deeply, smoothly and mindfully means being in touch with the total flow of life — inhale and exhale, holding on and letting go, gathering and giving, understanding and awe, living and dying. For the most part, humans are hardwired to 'do' and pursue, it is the art and practice of 'being' and letting go that requires our conscious attention and intention. This is the paradox of our nature – sometimes just being is the hardest thing to do.

□□

Live without guilt.
Own your life.

—

This is the life
the Creator gave you.

FORGIVENESS

□□

*M*ost people think of forgiveness as an act directed towards another, but forgiveness actually starts within yourself.

In order to move forward in life, we need to stop condemning ourselves for the innumerable actions (or non-actions) of our past and learn to forgive and accept ourselves with unconditional self-love and compassion.

Forgiving yourself is an essential ingredient in being able to forgive others. Not only that, forgiving yourself also helps to complete your past, so that it does not invade nor crowd your present. Incomplete projects or open files take up memory and real estate on your mental desktop, so to speak. As long as an experience or exchange is still running, without closure, it demands some sort of energy and awareness in the present moment, even if it happened years ago and you have stopped consciously thinking about it. Until you forgive, either yourself or the other party involved, the past is parasitically feeding off of your present.

To forgive does not mean to condone. We ought to rationally assess the choices we made in our past so that we can now, in the present, make more conscious, creative and compassionate decisions. In this way, our past becomes the seed for a better future by inspiring us to make better choices today. We learn from our past mistakes, and in this way, all of our tiny and epic failures are redeemed within the present moment. It is precisely because of our past that we have the appropriate energy, resources and perspectives in the present to make better choices and begin new patterns of positive behavior.

And yet, simultaneously, while we are making better and wiser choices in the present, we must recognize that everything in our past was in fact "meant to be," while the present and the future are both completely dependent upon our own free choice in the moment.

This is an essential perspectival paradox, a balanced equation of awareness that seeks to empower and inspire the individual in their quest for health, wealth and knowledge of self.

Restated in simpler terms:

The Past = meant to be, Divine Providence

The Present and Future = it's up to you, freewill and human agency

We are only truly forgiven when we let go of our foolish 'if only' daydreams — "if only" I did this or that, or, "if only" I was there and not here, etc. The past is done with and was meant to be, period!

The 'if only' mentality, say the mystics, is essentially heresy.

Once something happens it means that it was meant to be. It is only while something is in process that we have the opportunity to influence its outcome. It is, quite literally in that moment, up to us to steer the ship. Of course we never have complete control of the vessel, as there are always weather conditions and other ships out on the water that we have to respect and respond to. The most empowering perspective for the present (future included) is that everything is open to our input and conscious choosing; while the most liberating and healing perspective in relation to the past is that it was all meant to be, for reasons sometimes obvious and other times veiled in mystery.

Now, after we have examined the inner workings of forgiving ourselves, let us explore the mechanics of forgiving others.

In addition to learning how to forgive ourselves, it is equally important to learn how to forgive others, both for our own benefit as well as for the psycho-spiritual benefit of the other who has caused us pain. If someone has wronged you, although the ramifications of their actions may still trigger pain, it is ultimately up to you to open the channels of healing and reconciliation once they have taken the decisive step to ask for your forgiveness. Closing off the heart and carrying around a grudge can often be quite exhausting and even more burdensome than the original wound.

If we choose to go through life feeding the fire of our anger towards those who have hurt us, we end up carrying that negativity with us wherever we go, ultimately placing the power to choose a new future into the hands of the very people who have hurt us.

Forgiveness is the only way to release ourselves from an often all-consuming involvement with the offender (and the offense) that we feel we have suffered.

In Hebrew the word for joy/*simcha* contains the same letters that spell the Hebrew words *sh'emcha*/that erases. When we are able to untangle ourselves and thus 'erase' the negative effects of another person's (or even our own) negative actions, we then let go of our attachments to those crippling narratives that hold us back and keep us fossilized in the past. We are thus able to live in the present with more joy, awareness and freedom. Not only does forgiveness and its attendant 'erasing' result in joy, but, even more radical is the fact that cultivating joy, even in the midst of a struggle or conflict, can actually empower and allow one to forgive in the first place, as joy itself is "that which erases."

It should be pointed out that forgiving does not mean forgetting. It is often beyond our control whether we forget something or not; sometimes, in fact, we need to remember. Despite this, we should always do our best to forgive, as it benefits both us and any others who may have been involved in past situations of pain and estrangement. From this perspective, we are able to see that sometimes it is necessary to forgive although we may never be able to forget.

There is a marked distinction between forgiving and forgetting. It basically boils down to the fact that forgiving is selfless and pro-active, while forgetting is selfish and ultimately passive.

When we say to someone, "I have forgotten about it," we are essentially saying that their actions do not matter to us, and because of this lack of concern regarding them and their actions, we are able to move on. There is a hidden sense of self-importance and passive-aggressive anger in this attitude.

To forgive, on the other hand, is to selflessly move on with our lives, even if their actions did matter and even if their effects still cause us pain.

Forgetting is usually 'for-getting' something from the other person—namely a false sense of power. Forgiving, on the other hand, is 'for-giving' something to another—namely their freedom from your judgment. When you forgive, you may still be very much aware of the harmful actions or attitudes of the other, as well as your own feelings of loss, shame and hurt; yet you are able to rise above them in order to offer the transformative gift of forgiveness.

Do yourself and others in your life a favor, take back the power to choose and give them (and yourself) the gift of another chance.

□□

CULTIVATING
THE POSITIVE

Be aware of what you put out into the world,
as well as what you let in.

If you spend time around negative
and pessimistic people
it will have a damaging effect on you.

The converse is also true with positive,
optimistic and joyful people.

Choose whom you surround yourself with
— and when there is no option —
learn to create a protective shield.

THE POWER OF

Positive Thinking

□□

otwithstanding the snide and sarcastic cynicism that is in vogue today, there is a lot to be said for simple optimism. For one thing, the more you believe in something, the more you open yourself up to the possibility that it may occur.

That is not to say that positive thinking is the only thing required to manifest what we want in our lives. That is obviously an oversimplification. Our own hard work and self-sacrifice are required to create the space within which our dreams can be realized. On the other hand, it is safe to say that, self-defeating perspectives often stand in the way of us achieving our goals.

Hope, optimism and positive thinking can therefore play instrumental roles in preparing us for success.

On a simple level, as we begin to change, the world around us changes to match our frequency. At the very least, when we shift our perception of the world around us, we will shift the quality of the energy that we put out into the world, which is then reflected back at us. This is not a one-to-one formula or equation, as the world is not a predictable vending machine that will always give back exactly what we put into it; but it is at least a pro-active posture towards reality-curation, which in itself is empowering. In short, when we approach life with a positive mindset we will be more capable of locating and articulating 'the positive' in any given situation. This, in and of itself, is a form of redemption, one that we initiate through the focus and intention of our own consciousness.

Our minds are the interface between our internal selves and the external reality that is the world. Our internal perspectives are filters through which we affect, and are affected by, the external world. It may be said that good things happen to good people and negative things happen to negative people simply because good people experience what happens to them as good and negatively conditioned people experience what happens to them as negative. This is a perspectival twist on the common existential question of why bad things happen to good people. In this version, we are not referring to the ontology of what happens (i.e. whether what happens is objectively good or bad), instead we are focusing on the epistemology of how something is experienced (i.e. whether that which has happened is subjectively perceived and processed as being good or bad).

On a deeper level, our beliefs and convictions create our reality. This is the meaning of the Yiddish expression that states, "Think good and it will be good." Enough cannot be said regarding the power of positive thinking.

Furthermore, we find that people respond in kind, meaning that if we choose to smile and be joyous the people around us will, at least somewhat, be happier and more at ease around us. Conversely, when we choose to walk around angry, actively exuding negative energy, people will respond in kind. Thinking positive thoughts, and expecting to see positive results, attracts people and situations that resonate with this perspective. Conversely, entertaining feelings of hopelessness and despair calls forth situations and predicaments that will reinforce such a worldview.

We each generate an *ohr makif* surrounding light and energy around us in direct relation to our mindset. Positive thoughts, words and actions generate positively charged energy; the converse is also true. Whether consciously or subliminally we all pick up on these vibrations from those around us and respond accordingly. There is a natural tendency to gravitate toward those who feel good about themselves and radiate goodness, and to stay away from those who do the opposite.

On a larger scale, the macrocosm is a reflection of the microcosm; what flows from Above is a reflection of what is below. The absolute confidence and conviction in the Creator's goodness, becomes the vessel and conduit through which we draw down and receive that goodness. Expressed in Kabbalistic terminology: The shape and form of one's vessel affects the quality of the light that one is able to receive, and in turn, give over to others.

We achieve what we believe. This goes for the positive as well as the negative.

When we cultivate and nurture a positive outlook on life we will find that things work out for the good in the end. This often requires a more developmental or process-oriented view on events in life and history, especially considering that certain experiences are indeed painful or traumatic.

Notwithstanding the viewpoint expressed above (and this is an important point to stress), sometimes reality will not and does not change no matter how resiliently we maintain our positive perspective. Sometimes our challenges and sufferings, for reasons unknown to us, do not turn out for the better; whatever the reason may be, sometimes things just do not work out. And yet, it is still wise to keep in mind those repeated moments in the book of Genesis when the Creator exclaims in response to His own creation, "it is good!" Admittedly, not everyone will be comforted by such a faith-based idea. But for those with faith in the Creator's fundamental goodness, this passage is a powerful reminder that no matter what is happening and no matter how much it hurts, it is ultimately for a greater good, even if we cannot see or imagine what that might be.

Ultimately, life is good. This does not mean that there is no pain or suffering or that we can be oblivious to all the hurt and injustice in the world. It does indicate that when we live our lives from a positive perspective, our viewpoint itself creates a greater potential for real positive change in the world.

The way that we deal with pain is primarily a matter of attitude and perspective. If we dwell on the negative, and wallow in our own sorrow, our pain becomes suffering and will tend to linger on. Only by choosing to see the positive in life, can we honestly look back at the difficult times and see the positive potential hidden within those trying moments. It is by virtue of such a redemptive vision that we are able to see the hidden light within the darkness, and thereby understand how even those painful experiences have contributed to strengthening and refining our inner character. We can then look back at our negative experiences as a kind of tough-love obstacle course that was teaching us hard but necessary lessons. To perceive the past through this lens is to perform an alchemical act of inclusion and integration, for now all of our past experiences creatively contribute to who we have become, by helping us to evolve and become a more optimistic and hopeful human being.

A measure of deep inner joy and hopeful positivity is achieved when we realize, there are certain things in life that we can control and there are others things which we cannot. We have to learn to accept that certain things in our lives are beyond our control. Certainly we had no (conscious) control as to who our parents would be or into which culture and environment we would be born. So we need to stop spinning our wheels and spending our energy thinking, "what if I had different parents," or "what if my mother had really cared about me," or "what if this other person I really liked would have liked me back..." This type of thinking does no good and quite simply, just squanders energy that could otherwise be mobilized for making your life better in the moment, as well as in the future, rather than dwelling on the unchangeable aspects of your past.

And yet, even with regards to the things and people in our lives that we cannot change or control, we can at the very least control how we respond to them. This is the straight path towards inner joy—learning to take responsibility (the ability to respond) for the circumstances of one's life by consciously responding to them with mindfulness and intention, never allowing one's external situation to dictate how one feels internally about themself.

The stimuli of life are often outside the realm of your control, but your response to that stimuli *is* in your control and will ultimately impact your immediate and future set of circumstances.

A better future is dependent upon the decisions you make in the moment. Redeem your past mistakes and suffering by viewing life through a positive and productive lens in the present.

□□

It is not what you see in the world
that affects you, but rather how you see it.

Let go of your pre-conceived narrative
and learn to see things the way they are,
not the way you are.

THE POWER OF SIGHT
TO EFFECT CHANGE

□□

ow we see; namely—the perspectives, preferences and paradigms that we are running internally—affects *what* we see, namely—our interpretations and understandings of the sensations and situations that we encounter in the world.

The ancient philosophers argued ceaselessly about how we actually see things. There are two major theories. One states that in order for us to see a thing, a 'light' from that object is emitted and travels towards the viewer who then receives (sees) that light with their eyes. The second theory states that the viewer's eyes emit a 'light,' which then illuminates the external object. In other words, either the initiatory movement of sight/light is moving from object to subject (theory 1), or from subject to object (theory 2).

Empirical evidence suggests that "sense-objects" are received in the brain from object to subject. As you look at the words on this page for example, rays of light pass from the page to your eyes. These rays then register as an inverted (upside-down) image of the page on your retina. Light-sensitive cells cause impulses to pass through your optic nerve, leading to complex electrochemical patterns in your brain, which you process and finally interpret as a page (right side up) with words on it. This is a one-way path, from object to subject (theory 1).

But one thing still remains a mystery. Why do we perceive the image of the page as being 'outside' of us, when the image that we are actually seeing is appearing within our own brain?

If one were to perceive accurately, perhaps it would be more natural to say, "I am seeing a page in my mind," rather than, "I am seeing a page two feet away from my face." It is only our mental projection of the image outward, onto an assumed 'outside' world, that makes objects appear outside of our own mind. For this reason, while the original light of an object is certainly received by our eyes, it can also be argued that we then project the light of that vision outward, to be perceived. Thus, our minds extend themselves into the outside world, so-to-speak. In this way, there is also a visionary movement from subject to object (theory 2).

Taking this idea a step further, we enter into the realm of basic quantum theory, which states that the observer of a phenomenon affects the very thing that he or she is observing. As a result, the sharply drawn directional lines between subject and object become blurred. This paradigm of the "observer-effect" allows us to realize that we live in a radically inter-dependent universe/reality, in which, the perceiver of something is able to influence that which is being perceived through the very act of their perception.

Another mystery that needs to be understood is the fact that some people can accurately sense when an unseen person is staring at them. Here, not only does the seer (the unseen person) affect the seen (the one who can sense being stared at), but a seer 'out there' can seem to affect us 'in here,' meaning that they can impact our internal emotional and mental states just by the very *act of looking* at us.

The deepest truth is that the way we see things affects the very things we are seeing. For example, someone with pure intention emits a positive energy when looking at someone or something, and the opposite holds true as well. Our vision emits subtle vibrations into the universe directed towards the person/object we are viewing. We have all experienced this in the moment of a loving glance from a spouse, child, friend or parent; or, conversely, in the moment of a disapproving glare from a teacher, boss, or motorist that we have accidentally cut off on the road.

We do not see things the way they are, rather, we perceive things the way *we* are.

Furthermore, it is important to note that the "way we are" (i.e. our mindset and our state of consciousness) in the moment of observation, actually affects what we observe and can even alter the vibrational field of the person or thing itself. The act of looking at something can transform its energy from negative to positive, and vice versa, depending upon the quality of the seer's 'light' in the moment.

We should therefore be careful how we view things and how we interpret them, as our 'seeing' affects the quality of the very thing being seen.

When we see something negative we should take a moment of introspection, go back into ourselves where the 'light' is being absorbed in order to change its reflection, then project it back out to the world in a more positive hue. If we can imagine something as being wonderful and positive, we can then see it that way; when we see it in that light, it has a greater possibility of actually being exactly so.

When we view a person or an event in a positive light, we actually generate and project positive energy that can change the very nature of that person or event in the moment.

Our seeing affects what is being seen. When we see people in a positive light, and recognize their potential, they respond—much as a plant turns to the light—to be that which we see in them.

□□

To truly listen to
another person is
to grant them
their full humanity.

DEEP LISTENING

□□

One of the greatest gifts we can give another person is to truly listen to them, to be fully present and open to receiving their 'story.'

To speak is a Divine gift, to listen is itself Divine.

The ability to speak and share our thoughts, feelings and ideas is a spiritual quality that we as humans possess. This magical act is accomplished through the vehicle of words. But to listen to another person, to become the container and receiver of another person's life story, allows the listener to emulate a truly Divine-like quality.

THE POWER OF CHOICE

This redemptive gift is given through the medium of silence.

To listen to another is a wonderful art and, like all art forms, it needs to be cultivated and practiced. The more we practice listening, the more proficient and present we become.

For the purposes of this exploration, we will divide the concept of listening into ten levels within four different subcategories: physical, intellectual, soulful and transcendent. Each subcategory represents a deeper level of openness and unity, in relation to the other person to whom one is listening.

□

I. Physical Hearing:

1. Passive non-listening:

This is physical hearing at its most basic. Our ears are open, yet we are utterly apathetic and indifferent to the other person's words.

2. Active non-listening:

Deliberately ignoring the words spoken by the other and consciously rejecting the information entering our ears. This response may have value in certain situations, such as if someone is insulting or attacking you with demeaning words.

3. Pretending:

Showing outward signs of listening, yet inwardly blocking out or rejecting what is being spoken and heard.

4. Recording:

Mechanically accumulating what is being heard without absorbing meaning, similar to the inanimate functioning of a recording device or the rote memorization of a young student. In this case, there is still no real connection or relationship between speaker and listener.

In these forms of listening, receptivity is blocked by the static of self-centered judgment, anxiety or disinterest. There is no real relationship established with the other who is speaking.

□

II. INTELLECTUAL HEARING:

5. Projecting:

Hearing what you want to hear rather than what the other person actually has to say. Information has been received, but it is filtered through your own mentality or self-centered beliefs.

6. Manipulating:

This level takes 'hearing what you want to hear' to a deeper level, in which, the listener actively manipulates the other's words to say what he wishes to hear. It goes without saying that this can destroy a relationship.

This is the "i-it" paradigm of a relationship, in which, the listener objectifies the speaker as an object or "it" and uses his or her words for the listener's own self-serving purposes.

□

III. Soulful Hearing:

7. Attentive Listening:

Deep listening without mental static, self-projection or manipulation.

8. Empathizing:

Not only do you hear the words of the other person, you are actually open to them as a whole person, a unique entity. This allows you to perceive and understand the subtle meanings communicated through their tone, inflections and body language. You thereby begin to feel and respect where they are coming from. Essentially, you are in contact with the other person's soul.

This category of listening activates the "i-you" paradigm of real relationship. When we step out of our own way, we can truly be open to the heart of another. This is the beginning of deep listening where the listener creates a safe space for the speaker to openly articulate their struggles and challenges. The speaker feels safe sharing their troubles when they are heard on such a deep level. This kind of listening is a gift that helps to alleviate emotional burden. The mere act of listening on this level is a powerful method of healing.

□

IV. Transcendental Hearing:

9. Empowering:

Listening in a way that empowers the speaker's physical, emotional, mental and spiritual potential. For example, if someone asks you for advice, you trust that the answers they seek are already held within them. By letting the speaker tap into their own wisdom, you empower them to bring out their higher intuition. Both of you can then begin to sense the intrinsic unity between you.

10. Unifying:

On a deeper level of unity, your innate soul-powers actually transfer to the speaker and become manifest through them. For example, if you are naturally calm and the speaker struggles with issues of anger, your peaceful energy can actually flow into them through the process of your deep listening and soul-identification, giving them the added strength to overcome their challenge. This type of listening comes about through the recognition that there is really only One, and every 'i' is merely an expression of the Ultimate I.

This is the 'i-I' paradigm of relationship, which, in a sense, transcends 'relationship' altogether. On this level you become 'one' with the other person without losing yourself. Losing yourself completely in the other would not allow you to receive them or to offer any substantial or meaningful advice. However, at this level it is important to transcend your lower ego-self, otherwise you would not be able to truly hear the other as they are, but only as you perceive or project them to be. In this paradigm both parties, the speaker and the listener, sense their underlying unity within the Presence of the Ultimate I of the Creator. This is true listening.

Note: In this context it must be clearly stated that at no point are you actually offering the other person advice. The whole point of this practice is to just listen. Even when you are empathizing with the other you are not offering them your advice or perspective, as that would be contrary to the art of deep listening. If necessary, at a later time you can come back and offer them advice, but at this point you are really just listening. The goal of such a practice, of deep listening, is that through the very act of articulating their concerns, the speaker will become empowered to "hear" the answers they are seeking echo back from within. In this process, it is possible that the speaker might even need to draw upon your reservoirs of strength and wisdom to find their own answer. In such a situation your job is to be available, empathetic and supportive.

Parenthetically, if the other person is really pushing you to offer them advice, first you need to listen deeply on all levels and only after a moment of pause and reflection should you offer any advice. Internalize their issue, make it your own, and only then begin to answer.

Every word, letter or sound contains within itself the three primary dimensions of 'worlds,' 'souls' (or 'angels'), and 'Divinity.' Deep listening allows you to perceive these three dimensions simultaneously and also inclusively, enabling you to hear all three dimensions at once. It should be noted that the perception of one level does not cancel out the presence of the others. On the contrary, the awareness of one level may very well enhance your awareness of the other two.

'Worlds,' in the plural, alludes to the universal interconnectedness of all places, times and events. Awareness of this reality allows the listener to extrapolate what the speaker truly means, from what they actually said, based on archetypal analogy. When someone is speaking, you are able to listen deeply and hear 'worlds' within their words. This is the level of meaning.

'Souls' or 'Angels' alludes to hearing the deeper teaching within the other person's words. What is the lesson that is being imparted through their story? What can I receive from this message that relates to my life? This is the level of message.

'Divinity' implies the ability to sense that there is truly only One I. This leads to the understanding that every 'I,' both that of the speaker and that of the listener, is merely an expression of the Ultimate I, which is G-d. This is the level of monism.

When one deeply listens to another they can hear all three levels of expression as outlined above, and understand the multi-dimensional meaning of the speaker's words. As a result, they can detect the hidden messages encoded within the story and connect to the experience as a valid aspect of the Ultimate Unity, of which they are both a part.

We are all gifted with the wonderful ability to humbly receive the story and energy of another person, all we need to do is be present with an open heart.

*What makes us different
from robots is our ability to doubt.*

*The moment we stop asking questions
is the moment we cease being human.*

ASKING QUESTIONS
and
POSITIVE DOUBT

□□

I n order to constantly grow as human beings we should never feel as if we have arrived at our final destination. To move forward we should perpetually pose challenging questions to ourselves, and to the universe, as we seek ever deeper and higher answers to our most pressing concerns.

Questions are invaluable because they move us forward. If we are not moving forward, we are falling backwards; in life, there is no neutral. An answer on one level will eventually lead to another question on a higher level, which will then demand the further discovery of a new answer on an even deeper level.

You should never stop asking questions. The moment you stop asking questions, you are no longer being honest with yourself, and are therefore not truly alive. Living in a "knower" paradigm, in which you already have all the answers, leaves one feeling stale and stuck in routine. Ultimately, it means that one is living in a previously determined past, not in the infinitely unknowable present moment, which is full of surprises and novelty.

To live in the Tree of Life paradigm is to remain open to life and to the new.

Certainly, one should never feel bad for having questions. On the contrary, let your curiosity open you up to deeper and higher levels of creativity.

When we are not grounded in a commitment to a Higher Power, insecurity, fear and disorientation often result from our never-ending questions. But when we are firmly planted within the Ground of Being, our perpetually probing questions only lead us to more awe-inspiring insights.

Ideally, every answer leads to a deeper question and thus to a greater level of understanding. Each peak that we scale opens up to a wider panorama. Every thesis carries within it an antithesis, which calls forth a greater synthesis, until that synthesis itself leads to a new thesis, ad infinitum.

What satisfied our intellect yesterday may not and should not satisfy us today. We need to continually quest for deeper and higher meanings and messages related to our lives and the world as a whole; this we do by questioning. But is it really that simple? Are all questions created equal?

Many times people stop asking questions and start living life from a paradigm of predictability, where they already know all the answers. Perhaps, when they were younger they were full of questions, but they either did not get any good answers or were scolded to stop asking so many questions. This could have been the result of an insensitive, insecure, or impatient parent or teacher who was unable to keep up with their child's or student's curiosity, and thus attempted to "turn them off," so to speak. Or, this could have resulted from the particular way in which the questions were being asked. Perhaps the questions were just a child's way of challenging the authority of a parent or teacher.

Now it is time to start asking the real questions, the questions that are actually seeking answers. Be open to such questions, ask and ask again, go deeper and higher and your life will become richer and fuller.

Of course, doubt, uncertainty and unresolved issues can be crippling, but positive and productive doubt can free you and force you to investigate previously unexplored possibilities and perspectives.

Therefore, a distinction should be made between negative and positive doubt. This boils down to the difference between paradigms, in which, either nothing is possible or everything is possible. Negative doubt is crippling; it is an uncertainty in which you do not know what to do, and so you do nothing. Positive doubt is liberating; it creates a situation in which everything is possible.

Strong faith provides room for doubt. Faith of this sort will not crumble at the first sign of a challenge or contradiction that cannot be immediately explained. In fact, it will only be strengthened by being tested and questioned. Weak faith is unable to tolerate any doubt. This level of faith is incapable of entertaining any alternate viewpoint and, as a result, it is stuck in its own self-reinforcing circularity. It therefore does not have the capacity to evolve, expand or embrace more of reality.

From this perspective, a humble and honest question can be the source of positive doubt.

Have faith in the process. Never stop asking questions and always look for deeper answers.

□□

ABOUT THE AUTHOR

Rav DovBer Pinson is a world-renowned scholar, kabbalist, prolific author and beloved spiritual teacher.

He is widely recognized as one of the world's foremost authorities on authentic Kabbalah, philosophy & Jewish wisdom traditions and one of today's greatest living teachers.

Through his books, lectures and seminars, Rav Pinson has touched and inspired the lives of thousands the world over, and he continues to serve as a spiritual mentor and guide to many across the globe.

Rav Pinson has authored over 30 books, many of which have been translated into various languages including Hebrew, German, Spanish, Russian and Portuguese.

Rav DovBer Pinson is the Rosh Yeshiva of the IYYUN Kollel and heads The IYYUN Center in Brownstone Brooklyn, NY.

www.IYYUN.com